Keto Air Fryer Cookbook for Beginners

1800 Days of Quick, Easy, & Delicious Low Carb Recipes for Simple Weight Loss & Healthy Body. Includes 28-Day Ketogenic Diet Meal Plan for an Advanced Lifestyle

Amanda Ray

Table of Content

Introduction

Welcome to the Keto Air Fryer Cookbook for Beginners. As a professional nutritionist and culinary expert, I've created this book to guide you through the world of ketogenic cooking with the ease of an air fryer. Whether you're new to keto or looking for quicker, more efficient ways to prepare low-carb meals, this cookbook is your go-to resource for healthy, delicious, and convenient recipes.

The ketogenic diet, known for its high-fat, low-carb approach, helps your body enter ketosis, where it burns fat for energy instead of carbohydrates. Paired with the versatility of the air fryer, you can enjoy the crisp textures and rich flavors of fried food—without the excess oil or guilt.

This book simplifies keto principles into practical, flavorful recipes that anyone can prepare, even as a beginner. The air fryer makes cooking even easier, delivering meals that are crispy, tender, and nutrient-packed with minimal effort. Whether your goal is weight loss, improved metabolic health, or maintaining a low-carb lifestyle, this book ensures your keto journey is both enjoyable and sustainable.

Inside, you'll find a wide variety of recipes—hearty breakfasts, quick lunches, savory snacks, and satisfying dinners—designed to keep you aligned with your keto goals. Each recipe is low in carbs, high in healthy fats, and includes nutritional information to help you stay on track.

Beyond the recipes, you'll discover tips for maximizing your air fryer's potential, meal planning strategies, and guidance for maintaining your keto lifestyle with ease. You'll also learn about keto-friendly ingredients, cooking techniques, and how to avoid common pitfalls while following this dynamic diet.

Now, get ready to embrace a new way of cooking that combines the benefits of the ketogenic diet with the convenience of air frying. Let's begin your journey toward better health and delicious, crispy meals. Here's to your keto success!

Chapter 1: Keto and Air Frying - A Winning Combination

Welcome to the start of your keto and air frying journey! The ketogenic diet is a low-carb, high-fat way of eating that helps your body burn fat for energy. By combining it with air frying, you can enjoy delicious, crispy meals without the guilt of unhealthy oils or extra carbs.

Air frying lets you cook your favorite foods—like chicken wings, fries, and veggies—with less oil, making them healthier and perfect for keto. It's quick, easy, and gives you the fried flavors you love while keeping you on track with your keto goals.

In this chapter, I'll explore why keto and air frying are a great match and how they work together to make your meals both nutritious and delicious. Don't worry, I'll keep things simple and easy to follow. By the end, you'll be ready to start cooking tasty, keto-friendly meals with your air fryer! Let's get started!

What is the Keto Diet? A Simple Guide

The ketogenic diet, or keto, is a popular eating plan focused on reducing carbs and increasing healthy fats. Its primary goal is to help your body enter ketosis, where fat is burned for energy instead of carbohydrates. This can promote weight loss, balance blood sugar, and improve overall health, particularly for those with conditions like fatty liver disease.

In a typical diet, your body relies on carbohydrates—such as bread, pasta, and sugar—for energy. However, by cutting out most carbs, your body switches to burning fat, both from your diet and stored in your body. This can be especially beneficial for reducing liver fat in people with fatty liver disease.

The key to keto success is replacing high-carb foods with nutrient-dense, low-carb options that stabilize your blood sugar. This results in more consistent energy, fewer sugar cravings, and, most importantly for this cookbook, a reduction in liver fat.

Though the keto diet may seem restrictive at first, it's surprisingly flexible. You can enjoy satisfying meals, snacks, and even desserts while supporting your liver health.

In the next section, I'll explore Keto Myths, separating fact from fiction and provide tips to help you start on the right path. It's not about giving up the foods you love, but discovering new ways to enjoy them while taking care of your health. Let's dive into how keto can be a powerful tool for improving your liver and overall well-being!

Keto Myths: Separating Fact from Fiction

As with any popular diet, myths and misconceptions surround the ketogenic diet. It's crucial to separate fact from fiction, especially when considering its potential benefits for conditions like fatty liver disease. In this chapter, I'll debunk common keto myths and clarify what the diet truly offers.

Myth 1: Keto is Just Another Low-Carb Fad

Many assume keto is just another passing low-carb diet trend. While it is low in carbs, the core goal of keto is to induce ketosis, where your body burns fat for energy instead of carbs. This process is supported by science and offers numerous health benefits, including improved liver function, weight loss, and better blood sugar control. Unlike short-lived diets, keto has a well-established history of helping manage specific health conditions.

Myth 2: You Can Eat Unlimited Fat on Keto

A common misconception is that you can eat unlimited fat and still lose weight on keto. While healthy fats are emphasized, moderation is key. Focus on nutrient-dense sources like avocado, nuts, seeds, and olive oil. Consuming too much processed or unhealthy fat can lead to negative health outcomes, even if you're in ketosis. The focus should be on quality fats, balanced with protein and vegetables, to support overall well-being, especially when managing fatty liver disease.

Myth 3: Keto Will Damage Your Liver

This myth stems from the belief that a high-fat diet is harmful to the liver. In fact, when done correctly, keto can reduce liver fat, making it a useful tool for managing non-alcoholic fatty liver disease (NAFLD). By lowering carbs and focusing on healthy fats, keto promotes fat burning and reduces fat stored in the liver. Research shows that keto can improve liver health and function, making it an effective option for those looking to manage or reverse fatty liver disease.

Myth 4: Keto is Too Restrictive

Another myth is that keto is too restrictive to follow long-term. While it requires eliminating high-carb foods, keto still offers a variety of satisfying options, including meats, fish, eggs, non-starchy vegetables, and healthy fats. With proper planning and the right recipes, keto can be both sustainable and enjoyable. The benefits, such as reducing liver fat and improving overall health, make the effort worthwhile. Understanding the facts behind the keto diet will boost your confidence in incorporating it into your lifestyle, especially if you're working to improve liver health. Now that I've cleared up these misconceptions, let's explore how keto can help manage fatty liver disease and support a healthier, more vibrant life.

The Essential Keto Foods: What to Eat and What to Skip

Now that I've covered the basics of the keto diet and debunked common myths, it's time to dive into the core of keto: the food. Knowing which foods to include and which to avoid is crucial for optimal results, especially when managing fatty liver disease. In this chapter, I'll outline the essential keto foods and help you create meals that are both delicious and liver-friendly.

What to Eat on Keto

The keto diet focuses on low-carb, high-fat, and moderate-protein foods to maintain ketosis, where your body burns fat for energy. Here are the keto-friendly staples to include:

- **Healthy Fats:** Focus on whole, unprocessed sources like avocado, olive oil, coconut oil, and nuts. These fats provide energy and support liver health.
- **Meats and Poultry:** Opt for fattier cuts like chicken thighs or pork belly. Beef, pork, lamb, and turkey also fit keto guidelines while adding flavor.
- **Fish and Seafood:** Fatty fish like salmon, mackerel, and sardines are rich in omega-3s, promoting heart and liver health. Shrimp and crab are also excellent low-carb proteins.
- **Eggs:** Eggs are versatile, and packed with healthy fats and protein. Enjoy them boiled, scrambled, or in a variety of dishes.
- **Non-Starchy Vegetables:** Low-carb veggies like spinach, kale, broccoli, cauliflower, and zucchini are nutrient-dense and support liver health while keeping carbs low.
- **Full-Fat Dairy:** Cheese, butter, cream, and sugar-free yogurt provide fat and flavor but should be consumed in moderation to avoid overeating.
- **Nuts and Seeds:** Almonds, walnuts, chia seeds, and flaxseeds add fiber, healthy fats, and crunch. Watch portion sizes, as some nuts can be higher in carbs.

What to Skip on Keto

Certain foods are high in carbs and can disrupt ketosis, making it harder to burn fat and improve liver health. Avoid the following:

- **Sugary Foods:** Steer clear of candy, cakes, cookies, and sugary drinks, which spike blood sugar and contribute to liver fat storage.
- **Grains and Starches:** Bread, pasta, rice, and cereals are too high in carbs, even whole grains, which don't fit into a keto plan.
- **High-Carb Fruits:** Fruits like bananas, apples, grapes, and oranges are high in sugar. Opt for low-carb fruits like berries in moderation.
- **Starchy Vegetables:** Avoid potatoes, corn, peas, and carrots, which are high in carbs. Stick to non-starchy vegetables like spinach and zucchini.
- **Beans and Legumes:** Lentils, beans, and chickpeas, though healthy in other diets, are too high in carbs for keto.
- **Processed Foods:** Packaged snacks and processed meats often contain hidden sugars and unhealthy fats. Focus on whole, natural foods.

Let's move forward and discover how Air Fryer can make your Keto journey easier.

Air Fryer: How This Tool Can Make Your Keto Journey Easier

The air fryer has become a game-changer for making quick, delicious, and healthy meals, especially on the keto diet. This tool uses hot air to cook food, giving you a crispy, golden texture similar to frying but without excessive oil. For those managing fatty liver disease, the air fryer is a valuable ally, allowing you to create flavorful dishes that support both your keto goals and liver health.

Why the Air Fryer is Perfect for Keto

A key challenge of keto is enjoying rich, satisfying foods without relying on unhealthy fats. The air fryer solves this by cooking food quickly and evenly with minimal oil. You can still enjoy crispy chicken, crunchy vegetables, and keto-friendly fries without compromising your health. Using less oil means you're not overloading your meals with unnecessary fats, which is essential for liver care.

The air fryer also saves time, making it easier to stick to your keto plan. Whether preparing dinner or a quick snack, it cuts cooking time and offers a healthy, convenient option, perfect for busy days.

What Can You Cook in an Air Fryer?

The air fryer offers endless possibilities for keto meals. Here are a few ideas:

Crispy Chicken Thighs: Perfect for keto. Season with herbs, cook in the air fryer, and enjoy crispy skin with juicy, tender meat.

- **Vegetable Fries:** Zucchini, eggplant, and cauliflower can be made into low-carb fries. Toss with olive oil, season, and air fry until golden.
- **Keto-Friendly Snacks:** Make crunchy cheese chips, bacon-wrapped asparagus, or crispy pork rinds. The air fryer allows for easy, guilt-free snacking.
- **Fish and Seafood:** Salmon, shrimp, and scallops cook beautifully in the air fryer, with crispy exteriors and tender insides—ideal for keto meals.

How to Get the Most Out of Your Air Fryer

Maximize your air fryer's potential with these tips:

- **Use Minimal Oil:** A light spritz of olive or avocado oil is all you need for crispy results.
- **Avoid Overcrowding:** Give your food space to cook evenly. Overcrowding leads to soggy results, so let the hot air circulate.
- **Shake the Basket:** Shake the basket halfway through cooking to ensure even crisping.

By incorporating the air fryer into your keto routine, you can enjoy quick, flavorful, and liver-friendly meals with minimal effort. It's a simple tool that makes your path to better health easier and more enjoyable.

Combining Keto with Air Frying: Secrets for Success

Now that you're familiar with keto and the advantages of air frying, let's explore how to combine the two for maximum success. Using your air fryer to cook keto-friendly meals saves time while ensuring your dishes are flavorful and nutritious—crucial for managing fatty liver disease.

Here are some tips and secrets to help you get the most out of keto and air frying:

1. Focus on Healthy Fats

While the keto diet emphasizes fats, it's important to choose healthy options, especially for liver health. Oils like olive, avocado, and coconut oil are ideal for keto air frying since they withstand high temperatures and support ketosis while promoting liver health.

You don't need much oil when air frying—a light spritz or teaspoon brushed on food is enough to achieve a crispy, golden texture. This keeps your meals low in unnecessary calories while providing the benefits of healthy fats.

2. Choose Keto-Friendly Proteins

The air fryer excels at cooking keto-approved proteins like chicken thighs, salmon, and steak, sealing in moisture while creating a crispy exterior. Fattier cuts of meat, such as pork belly or beef ribs, cook well without the need for extra oils.

For quick meals, air fry sausages, bacon, or shrimp—these cook fast and are perfect for protein-packed snacks or meals.

3. Don't Forget About Vegetables

Low-carb vegetables like zucchini, cauliflower, and broccoli are keto staples and cook beautifully in the air fryer. Toss them in a bit of oil and seasoning, and you'll have crispy, flavorful veggies to pair with any meal. You can also make keto-friendly snacks like zucchini fries or kale chips, satisfying cravings without increasing your carb count.

Non-starchy vegetables provide fiber and nutrients without spiking blood sugar, which is essential for maintaining ketosis and supporting liver function.

4. Batch Cook for Convenience

Batch cooking is a game-changer for keto and air frying success. Cook multiple servings of chicken, fish, or vegetables and store them in the fridge or freezer for easy meals throughout the week. This saves time and ensures you always have healthy, keto-friendly options on hand.

Batch cooking makes sticking to your plan easier, especially on busy days when time is limited.

5. Season Smartly

Smart seasoning can elevate your keto air fryer meals. Fresh herbs, garlic, paprika, cumin, and other low-carb spices add depth without extra carbs. Avoid sugary marinades or pre-made sauces that may contain hidden sugars. Instead, create simple marinades with olive oil, vinegar, herbs, and spices.

Combining keto with air frying is a powerful strategy for improving health, especially for those managing fatty liver disease. By focusing on healthy fats, keto-friendly proteins, and low-carb veggies, you can create delicious, satisfying meals in minutes. With the convenience of batch cooking and smart seasoning, staying on track has never been easier.

Quick Tips for Keto Air Frying Beginners

As you start your keto air frying journey, it's normal to feel a bit unsure, but don't worry—air frying is simple. With a few easy tips, you'll be cooking delicious, healthy meals in no time. In this chapter, I'll share quick tips to help you master keto air frying, so you can confidently prepare crispy, flavorful dishes that support both your keto goals and liver health.

1. Preheat Your Air Fryer
Just like an oven, preheating your air fryer ensures even cooking and perfect crispiness. It only takes a few minutes, but it makes a big difference in how your meals turn out.

2. Use Minimal Oil
One of the best things about air frying is achieving crispy textures with little oil. Stick to healthy fats like olive, avocado, or coconut oil, but remember, a light brush or spritz is all you need to coat your food without adding unnecessary fats.

3. Avoid Overcrowding
For optimal results, avoid overcrowding the air fryer basket. Leave space for air to circulate, ensuring even cooking and crispiness. If you're cooking larger quantities, it's better to do it in batches rather than overcrowding the basket.

4. Shake or Flip for Even Cooking
About halfway through, shake the basket or flip your food to ensure even cooking on all sides. This works especially well for items like vegetable fries, chicken wings, or snacks.

5. Monitor Cooking Time
Air fryers cook faster than ovens, so keep an eye on your food. Some items may need less time, especially smaller or thinner cuts of meat. Check your food a few minutes before the recommended cooking time to avoid overcooking.

6. Season After Cooking When Needed
For certain foods, it's better to season after cooking, as spices can burn at high temperatures. Cheese crisps or delicate vegetables, for example, will taste best if seasoned immediately after cooking.

7. Clean Your Air Fryer Regularly
Regular cleaning keeps your air fryer in good condition and ensures your food tastes fresh. Clean the basket and tray after each use—most parts are dishwasher safe, making cleanup quick and easy.

8. Experiment with Different Foods
The air fryer is incredibly versatile, so don't hesitate to experiment with different keto-friendly foods like bacon, fish, veggies, and low-carb snacks. The more you try, the more confident you'll become in creating delicious meals. With these simple tips, you'll soon be a pro at keto air frying. Whether you're making crispy chicken, roasted veggies, or quick snacks, the air fryer is your go-to tool for healthy, delicious, liver-friendly meals. Now that you've mastered the basics, let's dive into some easy, tasty recipes to make your keto journey even more enjoyable!

Chapter 2: Breakfast

Cheesy Bacon Egg Cups

Time: 25 minutes	**Serving Size:** 6 egg cups
Prep Time: 10 minutes	**Cook Time:** 15 minutes

Nutrition Information Per Serving (1 egg cup):

Calories: 190, Carbohydrates: 2g, Saturated Fat: 7g, Protein: 12g, Fat: 16g, Sodium: 360mg, Potassium: 110mg, Fiber: 0g, Sugar: 1g, Vitamin C: 0mg, Calcium: 90mg, Iron: 1mg.

Ingredients:

- 6 large eggs
- 6 slices of bacon
- 1/2 cup shredded sharp cheddar cheese
- 1/4 cup diced green bell pepper
- 1/4 cup diced red onion
- 1/2 tsp garlic powder
- 1/4 tsp smoked paprika
- Salt and black pepper to taste
- Fresh parsley, chopped (for garnish)

Directions:

1. Preheat your air fryer to 375°F.
2. In a skillet, lightly cook the bacon slices over medium heat for about 3-4 minutes until they are slightly crisp but still pliable. Remove the bacon and set it aside.
3. In a medium bowl, crack the eggs and whisk them until smooth. Add the garlic powder, smoked paprika, salt, and black pepper to the eggs, and whisk again until well combined.
4. Grease a silicone muffin mold with a little oil. Line each cup with one bacon strip, forming a ring around the sides.
5. Add a sprinkle of diced green bell pepper and red onion to each bacon-lined cup for added crunch and flavor.
6. Pour the egg mixture evenly into each cup, filling them about three-quarters full.
7. Top each cup with shredded cheddar cheese.
8. Place the muffin mold into the preheated air fryer basket and cook for 10-12 minutes, or until the egg cups are set and the cheese is golden and bubbly.
9. Carefully remove the muffin mold from the air fryer and let the egg cups cool for a couple of minutes before removing them.
10. Garnish with freshly chopped parsley and serve warm for a flavorful keto breakfast.

Air-Fried Avocado Boats with Eggs

Time: 15 minutes	Serving Size: 2 avocado boats
Prep Time: 5 minutes	Cook Time: 10 minutes

Nutrition Information Per Serving (1 avocado boat):

Calories: 250, Carbohydrates: 6g, Saturated Fat: 5g, Protein: 9g, Fat: 22g, Sodium: 240mg, Potassium: 600mg, Fiber: 5g, Sugar: 1g, Vitamin C: 10mg, Calcium: 40mg, Iron: 1mg.

Ingredients:

- 1 large ripe avocado
- 2 medium eggs
- 1/4 cup crumbled feta cheese
- 1 tbsp chopped sun-dried tomatoes
- 1/2 tsp smoked paprika
- Salt and black pepper to taste
- Fresh cilantro or parsley for garnish
- Olive oil spray

Directions:

1. Preheat your air fryer to 350°F.
2. Slice the avocado in half and remove the pit. Use a spoon to scoop out a small amount of the avocado flesh from each half to create more room for the egg.
3. Lightly spray the avocado halves with olive oil and season the inside with salt, black pepper, and smoked paprika.
4. Carefully crack an egg into each avocado half, allowing the yolk to sit in the middle while the white fills the rest of the space.
5. Place the avocado boats in the air fryer basket, ensuring they are stable and upright. Air fry for 8-10 minutes, or until the eggs are cooked to your desired doneness.
6. Once cooked, remove the avocado boats from the air fryer and top each with crumbled feta cheese and chopped sun-dried tomatoes for added texture and flavor.
7. Garnish with freshly chopped cilantro or parsley and serve immediately for a nutrient-packed keto breakfast.

Keto Sausage Breakfast Balls

Time: 20 minutes	Serving Size: 8 balls
Prep Time: 10 minutes	Cook Time: 10 minutes

Nutrition Information Per Serving (1 sausage ball):

Calories: 180, Carbohydrates: 2g, Saturated Fat: 6g, Protein: 12g, Fat: 14g, Sodium: 360mg, Potassium: 150mg, Fiber: 0g, Sugar: 0g, Vitamin C: 0mg, Calcium: 50mg, Iron: 1mg.

Ingredients:

- 1/2 lb ground pork sausage
- 1/4 cup almond flour
- 1/2 cup shredded cheddar cheese
- 1/4 cup grated Parmesan cheese
- 1 large egg
- 1 tbsp chopped green onions
- 1/2 tsp garlic powder
- 1/4 tsp ground black pepper
- 1/4 tsp red pepper flakes (optional)
- Olive oil spray

Directions:

1. Preheat your air fryer to 375°F.
2. In a large mixing bowl, combine the ground pork sausage, almond flour, shredded cheddar cheese, Parmesan cheese, chopped green onions, garlic powder, black pepper, and red pepper flakes. Crack the egg into the mixture and mix well until everything is fully incorporated.
3. Form the mixture into 8 evenly-sized balls, ensuring they are packed tightly to maintain their shape during cooking.
4. Lightly spray the air fryer basket with olive oil and place the sausage balls in a single layer, leaving space between each one for even cooking.
5. Air fry for 8-10 minutes, turning the balls halfway through, until they are golden brown and cooked through.
6. Remove the sausage balls from the air fryer and let them cool for a minute. Serve warm as a keto-friendly breakfast option, or store them for meal prep throughout the week.

Zucchini and Bacon Fritters

Time: 25 minutes	Serving Size: 4 fritters
Prep Time: 10 minutes	Cook Time: 15 minutes

Nutrition Information Per Serving (1 fritter):

Calories: 150, Carbohydrates: 3g, Saturated Fat: 4g, Protein: 9g, Fat: 12g, Sodium: 350mg, Potassium: 180mg, Fiber: 1g, Sugar: 1g, Vitamin C: 10mg, Calcium: 40mg, Iron: 1mg.

Ingredients:

- 1 medium zucchini, grated
- 4 slices of bacon, cooked and crumbled
- 1/4 cup almond flour
- 1/4 cup grated Parmesan cheese
- 1 large egg
- 1/2 tsp garlic powder
- 1/4 tsp ground black pepper
- 1/4 tsp smoked paprika
- Olive oil spray
- Fresh parsley, chopped (for garnish)

Directions:

1. Preheat your air fryer to 375°F.
2. Place the grated zucchini in a clean kitchen towel and squeeze out as much moisture as possible.
3. In a mixing bowl, combine the zucchini, crumbled bacon, almond flour, Parmesan cheese, egg, garlic powder, black pepper, and smoked paprika. Stir until the mixture is well combined.
4. Form the mixture into 4 evenly-sized fritters. Ensure they are packed tightly so they hold their shape during cooking.
5. Lightly spray the air fryer basket with olive oil and place the fritters in a single layer, leaving some space between them.
6. Air fry for 10-12 minutes, flipping halfway through, until the fritters are golden brown and crispy on the outside.
7. Remove the fritters from the air fryer and garnish with freshly chopped parsley. Serve hot for a flavorful keto breakfast that's both crunchy and savory.

Almond Flour Pancakes

Time: 15 minutes	Serving Size: 4 pancakes
Prep Time: 5 minutes	Cook Time: 10 minutes

Nutrition Information Per Serving (1 pancake):

Calories: 210, Carbohydrates: 4g, Saturated Fat: 4g, Protein: 8g, Fat: 18g, Sodium: 150mg, Potassium: 70mg, Fiber: 3g, Sugar: 1g, Vitamin C: 0mg, Calcium: 60mg, Iron: 1mg.

Ingredients:

- 1 cup almond flour
- 2 large eggs
- 1/4 cup unsweetened almond milk
- 1 tsp vanilla extract
- 1/2 tsp baking powder
- 1/4 tsp cinnamon
- 1 tbsp coconut oil (melted)
- Olive oil spray
- Fresh berries and whipped cream for garnish (optional)

Directions:

1. Preheat your air fryer to 350°F.
2. In a medium bowl, whisk together the almond flour, eggs, almond milk, vanilla extract, baking powder, and cinnamon until a smooth batter forms.
3. Lightly grease a small air fryer-safe pan with olive oil spray.
4. Pour about 1/4 cup of the batter into the pan, spreading it evenly to form a round pancake shape.
5. Place the pan into the preheated air fryer and cook for 4-5 minutes, or until the edges are golden and the pancake is firm in the center.
6. Carefully flip the pancake using a spatula and cook for an additional 2-3 minutes until golden brown on both sides.
7. Repeat the process for the remaining batter, ensuring each pancake cooks evenly.
8. Serve the almond flour pancakes warm, optionally garnished with fresh berries and whipped cream for a delightful keto breakfast twist.

Chorizo and Egg-Stuffed Mushrooms

 Time:
20 minutes

 Serving Size:
4 stuffed mushrooms

 Prep Time:
10 minutes

 Cook Time:
10 minutes

Nutrition Information Per Serving (1 stuffed mushroom):

Calories: 180, Carbohydrates: 3g, Saturated Fat: 5g, Protein: 10g, Fat: 15g, Sodium: 390mg, Potassium: 290mg, Fiber: 1g, Sugar: 1g, Vitamin C: 2mg, Calcium: 40mg, Iron: 1.5mg.

Ingredients:

- 4 large portobello mushrooms
- 2 oz chorizo sausage, crumbled
- 4 large eggs
- 1/4 cup shredded mozzarella cheese
- 1/4 cup diced red bell pepper
- 1/2 tsp smoked paprika
- 1 tbsp olive oil
- Salt and black pepper to taste
- Fresh cilantro or parsley for garnish

Directions:

1. Preheat your air fryer to 360°F.
2. Clean the portobello mushrooms and remove the stems, brushing them lightly with olive oil on both sides. Season the mushroom caps with salt, black pepper, and smoked paprika.
3. In a skillet over medium heat, cook the crumbled chorizo for 2-3 minutes until browned. Add the diced red bell pepper and sauté for another minute.
4. Divide the cooked chorizo mixture evenly between the four mushroom caps.
5. Carefully crack one egg into each mushroom cap over the chorizo mixture.
6. Top the stuffed mushrooms with shredded mozzarella cheese.
7. Place the mushrooms in the air fryer basket and cook for 8-10 minutes, or until the eggs are set and the cheese is melted and golden.
8. Remove from the air fryer and garnish with freshly chopped cilantro or parsley. Serve hot for a protein-packed, keto-friendly breakfast option that's full of bold flavors.

Crispy Keto Hash Browns

 Time:
20 minutes

Serving Size:
4 hash browns

 Prep Time:
10 minutes

 Cook Time:
10 minutes

Nutrition Information Per Serving (1 hash brown):

Calories: 150, Carbohydrates: 4g, Saturated Fat: 3g, Protein: 5g, Fat: 12g, Sodium: 250mg, Potassium: 180mg, Fiber: 2g, Sugar: 1g, Vitamin C: 5mg, Calcium: 50mg, Iron: 1mg.

Ingredients:

- 1 medium zucchini, grated
- 1/2 cup shredded cheddar cheese
- 1/4 cup almond flour
- 1 large egg
- 1 tbsp grated Parmesan cheese
- 1/4 tsp garlic powder
- 1/4 tsp onion powder
- Salt and black pepper to taste
- Olive oil spray
- Fresh chives or parsley for garnish

Directions:

1. Preheat your air fryer to 375°F.
2. Place the grated zucchini in a clean kitchen towel and squeeze out as much moisture as possible to ensure the hash browns turn crispy.
3. In a medium bowl, combine the zucchini, shredded cheddar cheese, almond flour, egg, Parmesan cheese, garlic powder, onion powder, salt, and black pepper. Stir until everything is well mixed and forms a thick batter.
4. Divide the mixture into 4 portions and form them into round, flat patties.
5. Lightly spray the air fryer basket with olive oil and place the patties in a single layer.
6. Air fry the hash browns for 8-10 minutes, flipping halfway through, until they are golden brown and crispy on the outside.
7. Remove the hash browns from the air fryer and let them cool for a minute. Garnish with freshly chopped chives or parsley for added flavor and serve warm as a keto-friendly breakfast side.

Spinach and Cheese Omelette Bites

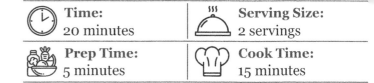 Time: 15 minutes	Serving Size: 6 omelette bites
Prep Time: 5 minutes	Cook Time: 10 minutes

Nutrition Information Per Serving (1 omelette bite):

Calories: 90, Carbohydrates: 2g, Saturated Fat: 3g, Protein: 6g, Fat: 7g, Sodium: 190mg, Potassium: 100mg, Fiber: 1g, Sugar: 0g, Vitamin C: 4mg, Calcium: 80mg, Iron: 1mg.

Ingredients:

- 3 large eggs
- 1/2 cup fresh spinach, chopped
- 1/4 cup shredded mozzarella cheese
- 1/4 cup grated Parmesan cheese
- 1 tbsp heavy cream
- 1/4 tsp garlic powder
- Salt and black pepper to taste
- Olive oil spray
- Fresh basil or parsley for garnish

Directions:

1. Preheat your air fryer to 350°F.
2. In a medium bowl, whisk together the eggs, heavy cream, garlic powder, salt, and black pepper until fully combined.
3. Stir in the chopped spinach, mozzarella, and Parmesan cheese, ensuring the ingredients are evenly distributed throughout the egg mixture.
4. Lightly spray a silicone muffin mold with olive oil and pour the egg mixture into each cup, filling them about three-quarters full.
5. Place the muffin mold in the air fryer basket and cook for 8-10 minutes, or until the omelette bites are set and slightly golden on top.
6. Carefully remove the muffin mold from the air fryer and allow the omelette bites to cool for a minute before popping them out.
7. Garnish with freshly chopped basil or parsley and serve warm for a delicious and keto-friendly breakfast packed with protein and leafy greens.

Cauliflower Breakfast Skillet

Time: 20 minutes	Serving Size: 2 servings
Prep Time: 5 minutes	Cook Time: 15 minutes

Nutrition Information Per Serving (1 serving unit):

Calories: 180, Carbohydrates: 5g, Saturated Fat: 4g, Protein: 12g, Fat: 14g, Sodium: 400mg, Potassium: 350mg, Fiber: 3g, Sugar: 2g, Vitamin C: 30mg, Calcium: 80mg, Iron: 1.5mg.

Ingredients:

- 2 cups cauliflower florets (fresh or frozen)
- 1/2 cup cooked sausage crumbles
- 2 large eggs
- 1/4 cup shredded cheddar cheese
- 1/4 tsp smoked
- paprika
- 1/4 tsp garlic powder
- Salt and black pepper to taste
- Olive oil spray
- Fresh parsley or cilantro for garnish

Directions:

1. Preheat your air fryer to 375°F.
2. Lightly spray the cauliflower florets with olive oil and season them with garlic powder, smoked paprika, salt, and black pepper.
3. Place the cauliflower in the air fryer basket and cook for 10 minutes, shaking halfway through to ensure even browning.
4. While the cauliflower is cooking, whisk the eggs in a bowl and season with a pinch of salt and black pepper.
5. After the cauliflower is done, transfer it to a skillet-safe dish or pan that fits into your air fryer.
6. Add the cooked sausage crumbles to the cauliflower, then pour the whisked eggs over the mixture, ensuring everything is evenly distributed.
7. Sprinkle shredded cheddar cheese on top and place the dish back into the air fryer. Cook for an additional 5 minutes, or until the eggs are set and the cheese is melted and golden.
8. Remove from the air fryer, garnish with freshly chopped parsley or cilantro, and serve hot for a keto-friendly, protein-rich breakfast.

Keto French Toast Sticks

Time: 15 minutes	**Serving Size:** 4 sticks
Prep Time: 5 minutes	**Cook Time:** 10 minutes

Nutrition Information Per Serving (1 stick):
Calories: 210, Carbohydrates: 4g, Saturated Fat: 6g, Protein: 8g, Fat: 18g, Sodium: 250mg, Potassium: 100mg, Fiber: 2g, Sugar: 1g, Vitamin C: 0mg, Calcium: 40mg, Iron: 1mg.

Ingredients:
- 2 slices of keto-friendly bread
- 2 large eggs
- 2 tbsp heavy cream
- 1/2 tsp vanilla extract
- 1/4 tsp cinnamon
- 1 tbsp butter (melted)
- 1/4 cup almond flour
- 1 tbsp powdered erythritol (optional, for sweetness)
- Olive oil spray
- Sugar-free maple syrup (optional, for dipping)

Directions:
1. Preheat your air fryer to 360°F.
2. Cut each slice of keto bread into 2 sticks, giving you a total of 4 sticks.
3. In a medium bowl, whisk together the eggs, heavy cream, vanilla extract, and cinnamon until well combined.
4. Dip each bread stick into the egg mixture, making sure it's fully coated.
5. In a shallow dish, mix almond flour with powdered erythritol. Gently roll each coated bread stick in the almond flour mixture to create a light crust.
6. Lightly spray the air fryer basket with olive oil and place the French toast sticks in a single layer.
7. Air fry for 8-10 minutes, flipping halfway through, until golden brown and crispy on the outside.
8. Remove from the air fryer and brush with melted butter for extra richness.
9. Serve warm with sugar-free maple syrup for dipping, or enjoy them as is for a delightful keto breakfast treat.

Air-Fried Veggie Frittata

Time: 20 minutes	**Serving Size:** 2 servings
Prep Time: 5 minutes	**Cook Time:** 15 minutes

Nutrition Information Per Serving (1 serving unit):
Calories: 180, Carbohydrates: 4g, Saturated Fat: 5g, Protein: 12g, Fat: 14g, Sodium: 300mg, Potassium: 250mg, Fiber: 2g, Sugar: 2g, Vitamin C: 20mg, Calcium: 100mg, Iron: 1.5mg.

Ingredients:
- 4 large eggs
- 1/2 cup spinach, chopped
- 1/4 cup red bell pepper, diced
- 1/4 cup zucchini, diced
- 1/4 cup shredded cheddar cheese
- 1 tbsp heavy cream
- 1/4 tsp garlic powder
- Salt and black pepper to taste
- Olive oil spray
- Fresh basil or parsley for garnish

Directions:
1. Preheat your air fryer to 350°F.
2. In a medium bowl, whisk the eggs together with the heavy cream, garlic powder, salt, and black pepper until well combined.
3. Stir in the chopped spinach, diced red bell pepper, zucchini, and shredded cheddar cheese.
4. Lightly grease an air fryer-safe dish or pan with olive oil spray, then pour the egg mixture into the pan, spreading it evenly.
5. Place the dish into the preheated air fryer and cook for 12-15 minutes, or until the frittata is set and slightly golden on top.
6. Remove the frittata from the air fryer and let it cool for a minute before slicing.
7. Garnish with freshly chopped basil or parsley and serve warm for a protein-packed, veggie-rich keto breakfast.

Ham and Cheese Egg Muffins

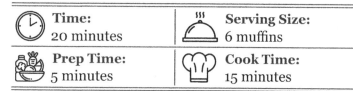

Time: 20 minutes	**Serving Size:** 6 muffins
Prep Time: 5 minutes	**Cook Time:** 15 minutes

Nutrition Information Per Serving (1 muffin):

Calories: 130, Carbohydrates: 1g, Saturated Fat: 3g, Protein: 10g, Fat: 9g, Sodium: 360mg, Potassium: 150mg, Fiber: 0g, Sugar: 0g, Vitamin C: 1mg, Calcium: 60mg, Iron: 1mg.

Ingredients:

- 6 large eggs
- 1/2 cup diced ham
- 1/4 cup shredded cheddar cheese
- 1/4 cup diced green onions
- 1 tbsp heavy cream
- 1/4 tsp garlic powder
- Salt and black pepper to taste
- Olive oil spray
- Fresh parsley for garnish

Directions:

1. Preheat your air fryer to 350°F.
2. In a medium bowl, whisk together the eggs, heavy cream, garlic powder, salt, and black pepper until smooth.
3. Stir in the diced ham, shredded cheddar cheese, and diced green onions, ensuring the ingredients are evenly distributed.
4. Lightly grease a silicone muffin mold with olive oil spray. Pour the egg mixture evenly into the muffin cups, filling each about three-quarters full.
5. Place the muffin mold in the air fryer basket and cook for 12-15 minutes, or until the egg muffins are set and slightly golden on top.
6. Carefully remove the muffin mold from the air fryer and let the muffins cool for a minute before removing them.
7. Garnish with freshly chopped parsley and serve warm for a quick and protein-packed keto breakfast.

Breakfast Sausage Patties

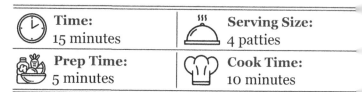

Time: 15 minutes	**Serving Size:** 4 patties
Prep Time: 5 minutes	**Cook Time:** 10 minutes

Nutrition Information Per Serving (1 patty):

Calories: 190, Carbohydrates: 1g, Saturated Fat: 5g, Protein: 12g, Fat: 16g, Sodium: 320mg, Potassium: 180mg, Fiber: 0g, Sugar: 0g, Vitamin C: 0mg, Calcium: 10mg, Iron: 1mg.

Ingredients:

- 1/2 lb ground pork
- 1/4 tsp garlic powder
- 1/4 tsp onion powder
- 1/4 tsp smoked paprika
- 1/2 tsp fennel seeds
- 1/4 tsp crushed
- red pepper flakes (optional)
- 1/4 tsp dried sage
- Salt and black pepper to taste
- Olive oil spray

Directions:

1. Preheat your air fryer to 375°F.
2. In a medium bowl, combine the ground pork with garlic powder, onion powder, smoked paprika, fennel seeds, crushed red pepper flakes (if using), dried sage, salt, and black pepper. Mix well until all the spices are evenly incorporated.
3. Divide the mixture into 4 equal portions and shape each into a round patty about 1/2 inch thick.
4. Lightly spray the air fryer basket with olive oil and place the sausage patties in a single layer, leaving some space between them.
5. Air fry for 8-10 minutes, flipping halfway through, until the patties are golden brown and fully cooked through (internal temperature of 160°F).
6. Remove from the air fryer and let them cool for a minute before serving. Enjoy these savory sausage patties as a perfect keto-friendly breakfast option.

Keto Breakfast «Burrito» Bowls

⏰ Time: 20 minutes	🍽 Serving Size: 2 bowls
🥗 Prep Time: 5 minutes	👨‍🍳 Cook Time: 15 minutes

Nutrition Information Per Serving (1 bowl):

Calories: 320, Carbohydrates: 5g, Saturated Fat: 7g, Protein: 20g, Fat: 25g, Sodium: 620mg, Potassium: 480mg, Fiber: 2g, Sugar: 2g, Vitamin C: 20mg, Calcium: 100mg, Iron: 2mg.

Ingredients:

- 4 large eggs
- 1/2 cup cooked ground sausage or chorizo
- 1/2 cup diced bell pepper (any color)
- 1/4 cup diced red onion
- 1/4 cup shredded cheddar cheese
- 1/2 avocado, sliced
- 1 tbsp sour cream (optional)
- 1 tbsp chopped cilantro for garnish
- 1/4 tsp garlic powder
- 1/4 tsp smoked paprika
- Salt and black pepper to taste
- Olive oil spray

Directions:

1. Preheat your air fryer to 350°F.
2. Lightly spray a small air fryer-safe pan or dish with olive oil.
3. In a medium bowl, whisk together the eggs, garlic powder, smoked paprika, salt, and black pepper. Pour the egg mixture into the prepared pan.
4. Add the diced bell pepper, red onion, and cooked sausage or chorizo on top of the eggs.
5. Place the pan in the air fryer and cook for 12-15 minutes, or until the eggs are fully set and lightly golden on top.
6. Once cooked, remove the pan from the air fryer and divide the egg mixture between two bowls.
7. Top each bowl with shredded cheddar cheese, avocado slices, a dollop of sour cream (if using), and freshly chopped cilantro for garnish.
8. Serve immediately for a delicious and filling keto breakfast that's inspired by burrito flavors—without the tortilla.

Air-Fried Salmon and Spinach Scramble

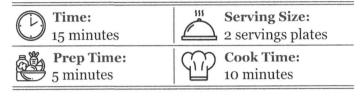

⏰ Time: 15 minutes	🍽 Serving Size: 2 servings plates
🥗 Prep Time: 5 minutes	👨‍🍳 Cook Time: 10 minutes

Nutrition Information Per Serving (1 serving plate):

Calories: 280, Carbohydrates: 2g, Saturated Fat: 4g, Protein: 24g, Fat: 19g, Sodium: 320mg, Potassium: 400mg, Fiber: 1g, Sugar: 1g, Vitamin C: 12mg, Calcium: 50mg, Iron: 2mg.

Ingredients:

- 4 oz salmon fillet (skin removed)
- 4 large eggs
- 1 cup fresh spinach, chopped
- 2 tbsp cream cheese
- 1/4 tsp garlic powder
- 1/4 tsp smoked paprika
- Salt and black pepper to taste
- Olive oil spray
- 1 tbsp fresh dill (optional, for garnish)

Directions:

1. Preheat your air fryer to 375°F.
2. Lightly spray the salmon fillet with olive oil and season with salt, black pepper, smoked paprika, and garlic powder.
3. Place the salmon fillet in the air fryer and cook for 6-8 minutes, or until the salmon is flaky and cooked through. Remove from the air fryer and set aside.
4. In a medium bowl, whisk together the eggs, cream cheese, and a pinch of salt and pepper.
5. Lightly spray a small air fryer-safe pan with olive oil, and pour the egg mixture into the pan. Stir in the chopped spinach.
6. Place the pan in the air fryer and cook for 4-5 minutes, stirring halfway through, until the eggs are softly scrambled and the spinach is wilted.
7. Flake the cooked salmon into bite-sized pieces and gently fold it into the scrambled eggs.
8. Garnish with fresh dill (if using) and serve warm for a nutritious, protein-packed keto breakfast.

Chapter 3: Appetizers and Snacks

Parmesan Zucchini Fries

Time: 20 minutes	**Serving Size:** 4 servings
Prep Time: 5 minutes	**Cook Time:** 15 minutes

Nutrition Information Per Serving (1 serving unit):

Calories: 120, Carbohydrates: 4g, Saturated Fat: 2g, Protein: 6g, Fat: 9g, Sodium: 250mg, Potassium: 350mg, Fiber: 2g, Sugar: 2g, Vitamin C: 10mg, Calcium: 100mg, Iron: 1mg.

Ingredients:

- 2 medium zucchinis
- 1/2 cup grated Parmesan cheese
- 1/4 cup almond flour
- 1 large egg
- 1/2 tsp garlic powder
- 1/4 tsp paprika
- Salt and black pepper to taste
- Olive oil spray
- Fresh parsley for garnish

Directions:

1. Preheat your air fryer to 375°F.
2. Cut the zucchinis into thin strips to resemble fries.
3. In a small bowl, whisk the egg and season with salt and black pepper.
4. In another bowl, mix the grated Parmesan cheese, almond flour, garlic powder, and paprika.
5. Dip each zucchini strip into the egg mixture, then coat it in the Parmesan-almond flour mixture, pressing lightly to ensure it sticks.
6. Lightly spray the air fryer basket with olive oil and place the coated zucchini strips in a single layer.
7. Air fry for 12-15 minutes, flipping halfway through, until the zucchini fries are golden brown and crispy.
8. Remove from the air fryer and garnish with freshly chopped parsley. Serve immediately for a crispy and flavorful keto snack or appetizer.

Bacon-Wrapped Jalapeño Poppers

⏰ Time: 20 minutes	🍽 Serving Size: 6 poppers
🥗 Prep Time: 5 minutes	👨‍🍳 Cook Time: 15 minutes

Nutrition Information Per Serving (1 popper):

Calories: 120, Carbohydrates: 2g, Saturated Fat: 4g, Protein: 6g, Fat: 10g, Sodium: 320mg, Potassium: 110mg, Fiber: 1g, Sugar: 1g, Vitamin C: 8mg, Calcium: 50mg, Iron: 0.5mg.

Ingredients:
- 6 large jalapeños
- 3 oz cream cheese, softened
- 1/4 cup shredded cheddar cheese
- 1/4 tsp garlic powder
- 6 slices of bacon
- Olive oil spray
- Fresh cilantro for garnish

Directions:

1. Preheat your air fryer to 375°F.
2. Cut the jalapeños in half lengthwise and remove the seeds and membranes.
3. In a small bowl, mix the softened cream cheese, shredded cheddar cheese, and garlic powder until well combined.
4. Fill each jalapeño half with the cheese mixture.
5. Wrap each stuffed jalapeño half with a slice of bacon, securing it with a toothpick if needed.
6. Lightly spray the air fryer basket with olive oil and place the bacon-wrapped jalapeños in a single layer.
7. Air fry for 12-15 minutes, or until the bacon is crispy and the jalapeños are tender.
8. Remove from the air fryer and garnish with freshly chopped cilantro. Serve immediately for a spicy and savory keto snack or appetizer.

Air-Fried Chicken Tenders

⏰ Time: 20 minutes	🍽 Serving Size: 4 tenders
🥗 Prep Time: 5 minutes	👨‍🍳 Cook Time: 15 minutes

Nutrition Information Per Serving (1 tender):

Calories: 180, Carbohydrates: 2g, Saturated Fat: 2g, Protein: 22g, Fat: 9g, Sodium: 320mg, Potassium: 270mg, Fiber: 1g, Sugar: 0g, Vitamin C: 0mg, Calcium: 30mg, Iron: 1mg.

Ingredients:
- 1 lb chicken tenders
- 1/2 cup almond flour
- 1/4 cup grated Parmesan cheese
- 1 tsp garlic powder
- 1/2 tsp smoked paprika
- 1 large egg
- 1 tbsp heavy cream
- Salt and black pepper to taste
- Olive oil spray
- Fresh parsley for garnish

Directions:

1. Preheat your air fryer to 375°F.
2. In a small bowl, whisk together the egg and heavy cream.
3. In another bowl, combine the almond flour, grated Parmesan cheese, garlic powder, smoked paprika, salt, and black pepper.
4. Dip each chicken tender into the egg mixture, then coat it in the almond flour mixture, pressing gently to ensure an even coating.
5. Lightly spray the air fryer basket with olive oil and place the coated chicken tenders in a single layer.
6. Air fry for 12-15 minutes, flipping halfway through, until the chicken tenders are golden brown and fully cooked (internal temperature of 165°F).
7. Remove from the air fryer and garnish with freshly chopped parsley. Serve hot for a crunchy and flavorful keto snack or appetizer.

Keto Buffalo Cauliflower Bites

Time: 20 minutes	Serving Size: 4 servings
Prep Time: 5 minutes	Cook Time: 15 minutes

Nutrition Information Per Serving (1 serving unit):

Calories: 110, Carbohydrates: 5g, Saturated Fat: 2g, Protein: 3g, Fat: 8g, Sodium: 400mg, Potassium: 250mg, Fiber: 2g, Sugar: 2g, Vitamin C: 30mg, Calcium: 20mg, Iron: 1mg.

Ingredients:

- 1 medium cauliflower head, cut into bite-sized florets
- 1/4 cup almond flour
- 1/4 cup grated Parmesan cheese
- 1/2 tsp garlic powder
- 1/2 tsp smoked paprika
- 1/4 tsp salt
- 1 large egg
- 1/4 cup buffalo sauce
- 2 tbsp melted butter
- Olive oil spray
- Fresh celery sticks and blue cheese dressing for serving (optional)

Directions:

1. Preheat your air fryer to 375°F.
2. In a small bowl, whisk the egg. In a separate bowl, combine the almond flour, Parmesan cheese, garlic powder, smoked paprika, and salt.
3. Dip each cauliflower floret into the egg mixture, then coat it with the almond flour mixture, ensuring an even layer.
4. Lightly spray the air fryer basket with olive oil and arrange the cauliflower florets in a single layer.
5. Air fry for 12-15 minutes, shaking the basket halfway through, until the cauliflower is golden and crispy.
6. While the cauliflower is cooking, mix the buffalo sauce with melted butter in a small bowl.
7. Once the cauliflower is done, transfer it to a large bowl and toss with the buffalo sauce mixture until well coated.
8. Serve hot with fresh celery sticks and a side of blue cheese dressing for a classic keto-friendly snack with a spicy twist.

Avocado Fries with Chipotle Mayo

Time: 20 minutes	Serving Size: 4 serving baskets
Prep Time: 5 minutes	Cook Time: 15 minutes

Nutrition Information Per Serving (1 serving basket):

Calories: 250, Carbohydrates: 8g, Saturated Fat: 3g, Protein: 4g, Fat: 22g, Sodium: 270mg, Potassium: 500mg, Fiber: 6g, Sugar: 1g, Vitamin C: 10mg, Calcium: 30mg, Iron: 1mg.

Ingredients:

- 1 ripe avocado
- 1/4 cup almond flour
- 1/4 cup grated Parmesan cheese
- 1/2 tsp garlic powder
- 1/4 tsp paprika
- 1 large egg
- Olive oil spray

For Chipotle Mayo:

- 1/4 cup mayonnaise
- 1 tsp chipotle powder
- 1 tsp lime juice
- Salt to taste

Directions:

1. Preheat your air fryer to 375°F.
2. Cut the avocado in half, remove the pit, and slice each half into fry-shaped wedges.
3. In a small bowl, whisk the egg. In another bowl, combine the almond flour, Parmesan cheese, garlic powder, and paprika.
4. Dip each avocado wedge into the egg mixture, then coat it in the almond flour mixture, ensuring an even coating.
5. Lightly spray the air fryer basket with olive oil and place the avocado fries in a single layer.
6. Air fry for 10-12 minutes, or until the fries are golden and crispy, flipping halfway through.
7. While the fries are cooking, mix the mayonnaise, chipotle powder, lime juice, and a pinch of salt in a small bowl to make the chipotle mayo.
8. Serve the avocado fries hot, paired with the chipotle mayo for dipping, for a rich, flavorful keto snack.

Garlic Butter Shrimp Skewers

Time: 15 minutes	Serving Size: 4 skewers
Prep Time: 5 minutes	Cook Time: 10 minutes

Nutrition Information Per Serving (1 skewer):

Calories: 180, Carbohydrates: 1g, Saturated Fat: 5g, Protein: 20g, Fat: 10g, Sodium: 450mg, Potassium: 150mg, Fiber: 0g, Sugar: 0g, Vitamin C: 4mg, Calcium: 90mg, Iron: 1mg.

Ingredients:

- 1 lb large shrimp, peeled and deveined
- 3 tbsp unsalted butter, melted
- 3 cloves garlic, minced
- 1 tbsp fresh lemon juice
- 1/4 tsp smoked paprika
- 1/4 tsp salt
- 1/4 tsp black pepper
- Fresh parsley for garnish
- Wooden skewers, soaked in water

Directions:

1. Preheat your air fryer to 370°F.
2. In a small bowl, combine the melted butter, minced garlic, lemon juice, smoked paprika, salt, and black pepper.
3. Thread the shrimp onto the soaked skewers, about 4-5 shrimp per skewer.
4. Brush the shrimp with the garlic butter mixture, ensuring they are evenly coated.
5. Lightly spray the air fryer basket with olive oil and place the skewers in a single layer.
6. Air fry for 8-10 minutes, flipping halfway through, until the shrimp are pink and cooked through.
7. Remove the shrimp skewers from the air fryer and garnish with freshly chopped parsley.
8. Serve hot as a delicious and keto-friendly appetizer or snack.

Crispy Keto Mozzarella Sticks

Time: 25 minutes	Serving Size: 6 sticks
Prep Time: 10 minutes	Cook Time: 15 minutes

Nutrition Information Per Serving (1 stick):

Calories: 140, Carbohydrates: 2g, Saturated Fat: 5g, Protein: 9g, Fat: 11g, Sodium: 240mg, Potassium: 60mg, Fiber: 1g, Sugar: 0g, Vitamin C: 0mg, Calcium: 200mg, Iron: 0.5mg.

Ingredients:

- 6 mozzarella cheese sticks (string cheese)
- 1/2 cup almond flour
- 1/4 cup grated Parmesan cheese
- 1/2 tsp garlic powder
- 1/2 tsp Italian seasoning
- 1/4 tsp salt
- 1 large egg
- Olive oil spray
- Sugar-free marinara sauce for dipping (optional)

Directions:

1. Preheat your air fryer to 360°F.
2. In a small bowl, whisk the egg. In a separate bowl, mix the almond flour, grated Parmesan cheese, garlic powder, Italian seasoning, and salt.
3. Cut each mozzarella stick in half, giving you 12 smaller sticks.
4. Dip each mozzarella stick into the egg mixture, then coat it in the almond flour mixture, ensuring an even layer. For extra crispiness, dip the coated sticks back into the egg and almond flour mixture again for a second coating.
5. Place the coated mozzarella sticks on a parchment-lined baking sheet and freeze for at least 1 hour to prevent melting in the air fryer.
6. Lightly spray the air fryer basket with olive oil and place the frozen mozzarella sticks in a single layer.
7. Air fry for 8-10 minutes, turning halfway through, until golden brown and crispy.
8. Serve hot with sugar-free marinara sauce for a delicious keto-friendly appetizer or snack.

Keto Cheddar Biscuits

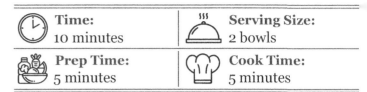

	Time: 20 minutes		Serving Size: 6 biscuits
	Prep Time: 5 minutes		Cook Time: 15 minutes

Nutrition Information Per Serving (1 biscuit):

Calories: 150, Carbohydrates: 3g, Saturated Fat: 5g, Protein: 8g, Fat: 12g, Sodium: 300mg, Potassium: 40mg, Fiber: 2g, Sugar: 0g, Vitamin C: 0mg, Calcium: 120mg, Iron: 0.8mg.

Ingredients:

- 1 cup almond flour
- 1/2 cup shredded sharp cheddar cheese
- 1/4 cup grated Parmesan cheese
- 1 large egg
- 2 tbsp unsalted butter, melted
- 1/2 tsp garlic powder
- 1/2 tsp baking powder
- 1/4 tsp salt
- Olive oil spray
- Fresh parsley for garnish (optional)

Directions:

1. Preheat your air fryer to 350°F.
2. In a medium bowl, mix the almond flour, shredded cheddar cheese, Parmesan cheese, garlic powder, baking powder, and salt.
3. In a separate small bowl, whisk the egg and melted butter together until well combined.
4. Pour the egg mixture into the almond flour mixture and stir until a thick dough forms.
5. Divide the dough into 6 equal portions and shape them into small round biscuits.
6. Lightly spray the air fryer basket with olive oil and place the biscuits in a single layer, leaving space between them.
7. Air fry for 10-12 minutes, or until the biscuits are golden brown and firm to the touch.
8. Remove from the air fryer and garnish with freshly chopped parsley, if desired. Serve warm as a delicious keto-friendly appetizer or snack.

Air-Fried Kale Chips

	Time: 10 minutes		Serving Size: 2 bowls
	Prep Time: 5 minutes		Cook Time: 5 minutes

Nutrition Information Per Serving (1 bowl):

Calories: 70, Carbohydrates: 6g, Saturated Fat: 1g, Protein: 3g, Fat: 4g, Sodium: 220mg, Potassium: 350mg, Fiber: 2g, Sugar: 1g, Vitamin C: 50mg, Calcium: 90mg, Iron: 1.2mg.

Ingredients:

- 2 cups kale leaves, stems removed and torn into bite-sized pieces
- 1 tbsp olive oil
- 1/4 tsp garlic powder
- 1/4 tsp smoked paprika
- Salt and black pepper to taste
- 1 tbsp grated Parmesan cheese (optional)

Directions:

1. Preheat your air fryer to 350°F.
2. In a large bowl, toss the kale leaves with olive oil, garlic powder, smoked paprika, salt, and black pepper until evenly coated.
3. Lightly spray the air fryer basket with olive oil and spread the kale leaves in a single layer.
4. Air fry for 4-5 minutes, shaking the basket halfway through, until the kale is crispy but not burnt.
5. Remove from the air fryer and sprinkle with grated Parmesan cheese if desired.
6. Serve immediately for a crunchy and nutrient-packed keto snack.

Cauliflower and Bacon Mini Tacos

 Time:
20 minutes

 Serving Size:
4 mini tacos

 Prep Time:
5 minutes

 Cook Time:
15 minutes

Nutrition Information Per Serving (1 mini taco):

Calories: 120, Carbohydrates: 3g, Saturated Fat: 3g, Protein: 7g, Fat: 9g, Sodium: 350mg, Potassium: 150mg, Fiber: 1g, Sugar: 1g, Vitamin C: 10mg, Calcium: 40mg, Iron: 0.7mg.

Ingredients:

- 1 cup cauliflower florets, finely chopped
- 4 slices of bacon, cooked and crumbled
- 1/4 cup shredded cheddar cheese
- 1 tbsp almond flour
- 1 large egg
- 1/4 tsp garlic powder
- 1/4 tsp paprika
- Salt and black pepper to taste
- Olive oil spray
- Fresh cilantro and sour cream for garnish (optional)

Directions:

1. Preheat your air fryer to 375°F.
2. In a medium bowl, combine the finely chopped cauliflower, crumbled bacon, shredded cheddar cheese, almond flour, egg, garlic powder, paprika, salt, and black pepper. Mix until everything is well combined.
3. Form the mixture into small, round, taco-shaped discs (about 4-5 inches in diameter).
4. Lightly spray the air fryer basket with olive oil and place the cauliflower taco shells in a single layer.
5. Air fry for 8-10 minutes, flipping halfway through, until the shells are golden and firm.
6. Once cooked, fill each mini taco shell with a bit more crumbled bacon and any optional toppings such as fresh cilantro or a dollop of sour cream.
7. Serve warm for a fun, crispy, and keto-friendly snack or appetizer.

Spicy Air-Fried Pickle Chips

 Time:
15 minutes

 Serving Size:
4 servings

 Prep Time:
5 minutes

 Cook Time:
10 minutes

Nutrition Information Per Serving (1 serving unit):

Calories: 90, Carbohydrates: 3g, Saturated Fat: 2g, Protein: 4g, Fat: 7g, Sodium: 350mg, Potassium: 60mg, Fiber: 1g, Sugar: 1g, Vitamin C: 1mg, Calcium: 40mg, Iron: 0.5mg.

Ingredients:

- 1 cup dill pickle chips (drained and patted dry)
- 1/2 cup almond flour
- 1/4 cup grated Parmesan cheese
- 1 large egg
- 1/2 tsp cayenne pepper (adjust to taste)
- 1/2 tsp garlic powder
- 1/4 tsp paprika
- Olive oil spray
- Ranch dressing or sugar-free dipping sauce (optional)

Directions:

1. Preheat your air fryer to 375°F.
2. In a small bowl, whisk the egg. In a separate bowl, combine the almond flour, Parmesan cheese, cayenne pepper, garlic powder, and paprika.
3. Dip each pickle chip into the egg mixture, then coat it with the almond flour mixture, pressing gently to ensure the coating sticks.
4. Lightly spray the air fryer basket with olive oil and place the coated pickle chips in a single layer.
5. Air fry for 8-10 minutes, flipping halfway through, until the pickle chips are golden brown and crispy.
6. Serve hot with a side of ranch dressing or your favorite sugar-free dipping sauce for a spicy, tangy, and keto-friendly snack.

Keto Eggplant Fries

🕐 Time: 20 minutes	🍽 Serving Size: 4 servings
🥗 Prep Time: 5 minutes	👨‍🍳 Cook Time: 15 minutes

Nutrition Information Per Serving (1 serving):

Calories: 120, Carbohydrates: 6g, Saturated Fat: 2g, Protein: 4g, Fat: 9g, Sodium: 320mg, Potassium: 250mg, Fiber: 3g, Sugar: 2g, Vitamin C: 2mg, Calcium: 50mg, Iron: 1mg.

Ingredients:

- 1 medium eggplant, cut into fry-sized sticks
- 1/2 cup almond flour
- 1/4 cup grated Parmesan cheese
- 1 large egg
- 1/2 tsp garlic powder
- 1/4 tsp smoked paprika
- Salt and black pepper to taste
- Olive oil spray
- Fresh parsley for garnish (optional)

Directions:

1. Preheat your air fryer to 375°F.
2. In a small bowl, whisk the egg. In another bowl, combine the almond flour, Parmesan cheese, garlic powder, smoked paprika, salt, and black pepper.
3. Dip each eggplant stick into the egg mixture, then coat it in the almond flour mixture, pressing gently to ensure even coverage.
4. Lightly spray the air fryer basket with olive oil and arrange the coated eggplant sticks in a single layer.
5. Air fry for 12-15 minutes, flipping halfway through, until golden brown and crispy.
6. Remove the eggplant fries from the air fryer and garnish with freshly chopped parsley if desired. Serve hot as a keto-friendly appetizer or snack.

Cream Cheese Stuffed Mini Bell Peppers

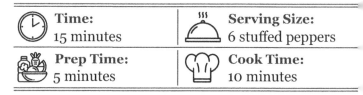

🕐 Time: 15 minutes	🍽 Serving Size: 6 stuffed peppers
🥗 Prep Time: 5 minutes	👨‍🍳 Cook Time: 10 minutes

Nutrition Information Per Serving (1 stuffed pepper):

Calories: 90, Carbohydrates: 3g, Saturated Fat: 4g, Protein: 2g, Fat: 8g, Sodium: 130mg, Potassium: 120mg, Fiber: 1g, Sugar: 2g, Vitamin C: 40mg, Calcium: 40mg, Iron: 0.2mg.

Ingredients:

- 6 mini bell peppers, halved and seeds removed
- 4 oz cream cheese, softened
- 1/4 cup shredded cheddar cheese
- 1/2 tsp garlic powder
- 1/4 tsp smoked paprika
- Salt and black pepper to taste
- Olive oil spray
- Fresh parsley for garnish (optional)

Directions:

1. Preheat your air fryer to 350°F.
2. In a small bowl, mix the softened cream cheese, shredded cheddar cheese, garlic powder, smoked paprika, salt, and black pepper until well combined.
3. Spoon the cream cheese mixture into each halved mini bell pepper, filling them generously.
4. Lightly spray the air fryer basket with olive oil and place the stuffed peppers in a single layer.
5. Air fry for 8-10 minutes, or until the peppers are tender and the cheese is melted and bubbly.
6. Remove from the air fryer and garnish with freshly chopped parsley if desired. Serve hot for a creamy, keto-friendly appetizer or snack.

Air-Fried Pork Belly Crisps

⏲ Time: 25 minutes	🍽 Serving Size: 4 servings
🥗 Prep Time: 5 minutes	👨‍🍳 Cook Time: 20 minutes

Nutrition Information Per Serving (1 serving unit):

Calories: 290, Carbohydrates: 0g, Saturated Fat: 10g, Protein: 10g, Fat: 26g, Sodium: 480mg, Potassium: 180mg, Fiber: 0g, Sugar: 0g, Vitamin C: 0mg, Calcium: 10mg, Iron: 0.8mg.

Ingredients:
- 1 lb pork belly, thinly sliced
- 1/2 tsp garlic powder
- 1/2 tsp smoked paprika
- 1/4 tsp black pepper
- 1/4 tsp salt
- Olive oil spray
- Fresh parsley for garnish (optional)

Directions:
1. Preheat your air fryer to 375°F.
2. In a small bowl, mix together the garlic powder, smoked paprika, black pepper, and salt.
3. Rub the spice mixture evenly over the pork belly slices.
4. Lightly spray the air fryer basket with olive oil. Arrange the pork belly slices in a single layer in the air fryer basket, ensuring they do not overlap.
5. Air fry for 18-20 minutes, flipping halfway through, until the pork belly is crispy and golden brown.
6. Remove the pork belly crisps from the air fryer and place them on a paper towel to absorb any excess oil.
7. Garnish with freshly chopped parsley if desired. Serve hot as a crunchy, savory, keto-friendly snack or appetizer.

Spinach and Artichoke Air-Fried Balls

⏲ Time: 20 minutes	🍽 Serving Size: 8 balls
🥗 Prep Time: 10 minutes	👨‍🍳 Cook Time: 10 minutes

Nutrition Information Per Serving (1 ball):

Calories: 90, Carbohydrates: 3g, Saturated Fat: 3g, Protein: 4g, Fat: 7g, Sodium: 250mg, Potassium: 120mg, Fiber: 1g, Sugar: 1g, Vitamin C: 5mg, Calcium: 80mg, Iron: 1mg.

Ingredients:
- 1 cup fresh spinach, chopped
- 1/2 cup canned artichoke hearts, drained and chopped
- 1/2 cup shredded mozzarella cheese
- 1/4 cup grated Parmesan cheese
- 2 tbsp almond flour
- 1 large egg
- 1/2 tsp garlic powder
- 1/4 tsp black pepper
- 1/4 tsp salt
- Olive oil spray

Directions:
1. Preheat your air fryer to 360°F.
2. In a medium bowl, combine the chopped spinach, artichoke hearts, mozzarella cheese, Parmesan cheese, almond flour, egg, garlic powder, salt, and black pepper. Mix until well combined.
3. Form the mixture into 8 evenly-sized balls.
4. Lightly spray the air fryer basket with olive oil and arrange the balls in a single layer.
5. Air fry for 8-10 minutes, flipping halfway through, until the balls are golden brown and slightly crispy on the outside.
6. Remove from the air fryer and let them cool for a minute before serving. Enjoy these savory, keto-friendly spinach and artichoke balls as a delicious appetizer or snack.

Chapter 4: Poultry

Herb-Crusted Chicken Thighs

 Time:
35 minutes

 Serving Size:
4 chicken thighs

 Prep Time:
10 minutes

 Cook Time:
25 minutes

Nutrition Information Per Serving (1 chicken thigh):

Calories: 290, Carbohydrates: 2g, Saturated Fat: 4g, Protein: 23g, Fat: 20g, Sodium: 380mg, Potassium: 250mg, Fiber: 0g, Sugar: 0g, Vitamin C: 1mg, Calcium: 30mg, Iron: 1mg.

Ingredients:

- 4 bone-in, skin-on chicken thighs
- 2 tbsp olive oil
- 1/4 cup almond flour
- 1/4 cup grated Parmesan cheese
- 1 tbsp fresh parsley, chopped
- 1 tbsp fresh rosemary, chopped
- 1 tsp garlic powder
- 1/2 tsp smoked paprika
- 1/2 tsp salt
- 1/4 tsp black pepper

Directions:

1. Preheat your air fryer to 375°F.
2. In a small bowl, mix the almond flour, Parmesan cheese, parsley, rosemary, garlic powder, smoked paprika, salt, and black pepper.
3. Pat the chicken thighs dry with a paper towel and rub them with olive oil.
4. Press the herb and almond flour mixture onto the chicken thighs, coating them evenly.
5. Lightly spray the air fryer basket with olive oil and place the chicken thighs in a single layer, skin side up.
6. Air fry for 20-25 minutes, flipping halfway through, until the chicken reaches an internal temperature of 165°F and the skin is crispy and golden.
7. Remove the chicken from the air fryer and let it rest for a few minutes before serving. Enjoy these juicy, herb-crusted chicken thighs as a flavorful and keto-friendly poultry dish.

Air-Fried Chicken Drumsticks

 Time:
30 minutes

 Serving Size:
4 drumsticks

 Prep Time:
5 minutes

 Cook Time:
25 minutes

Nutrition Information Per Serving (1 drumstick):

Calories: 220, Carbohydrates: 1g, Saturated Fat: 4g, Protein: 21g, Fat: 15g, Sodium: 350mg, Potassium: 220mg, Fiber: 0g, Sugar: 0g, Vitamin C: 0mg, Calcium: 20mg, Iron: 1mg.

Ingredients:

- 4 chicken drumsticks
- 2 tbsp olive oil
- 1/4 cup almond flour
- 1/4 cup grated Parmesan cheese
- 1 tsp garlic powder
- 1 tsp smoked paprika
- 1/2 tsp onion powder
- 1/2 tsp salt
- 1/4 tsp black pepper

Directions:

1. Preheat your air fryer to 375°F.
2. In a small bowl, mix together the almond flour, Parmesan cheese, garlic powder, smoked paprika, onion powder, salt, and black pepper.
3. Pat the chicken drumsticks dry with a paper towel and rub them with olive oil.
4. Dredge each drumstick in the almond flour mixture, pressing the coating onto the chicken to ensure it sticks.
5. Lightly spray the air fryer basket with olive oil and place the drumsticks in a single layer.
6. Air fry for 22-25 minutes, flipping halfway through, until the drumsticks are golden brown and reach an internal temperature of 165°F.
7. Remove the drumsticks from the air fryer and let them rest for a few minutes before serving. Enjoy these crispy, flavorful chicken drumsticks as a keto-friendly poultry dish.

Keto Chicken Parmesan

 Time:
25 minutes

 Serving Size:
2 chicken breasts

 Prep Time:
5 minutes

 Cook Time:
20 minutes

Nutrition Information Per Serving (1 chicken breast):

Calories: 320, Carbohydrates: 4g, Saturated Fat: 6g, Protein: 36g, Fat: 18g, Sodium: 560mg, Potassium: 480mg, Fiber: 1g, Sugar: 2g, Vitamin C: 4mg, Calcium: 200mg, Iron: 1mg.

Ingredients:

- 2 boneless, skinless chicken breasts
- 1/2 cup almond flour
- 1/4 cup grated Parmesan cheese
- 1 tsp garlic powder
- 1 tsp Italian seasoning
- 1 large egg
- 1/2 cup sugar-free marinara sauce
- 1/2 cup shredded mozzarella cheese
- 1 tbsp olive oil
- Salt and black pepper to taste
- Fresh basil for garnish (optional)

Directions:

1. Preheat your air fryer to 375°F.
2. In a shallow bowl, whisk the egg. In another bowl, combine the almond flour, Parmesan cheese, garlic powder, Italian seasoning, salt, and black pepper.
3. Dip each chicken breast into the egg mixture, then coat it in the almond flour mixture, pressing firmly to ensure the coating sticks.
4. Lightly spray the air fryer basket with olive oil and place the coated chicken breasts in a single layer.
5. Air fry for 15 minutes, flipping halfway through, until the chicken reaches an internal temperature of 165°F and is golden brown.
6. Remove the chicken from the air fryer and top each breast with 1/4 cup of sugar-free marinara sauce and 1/4 cup of shredded mozzarella cheese.
7. Return the chicken to the air fryer and cook for an additional 3-5 minutes, or until the cheese is melted and bubbly.
8. Garnish with fresh basil and serve hot for a delicious keto-friendly twist on classic chicken Parmesan.

Crispy Lemon Garlic Chicken Wings

🕐 Time: 30 minutes	🍽 Serving Size: 4 servings
🥗 Prep Time: 5 minutes	👨‍🍳 Cook Time: 25 minutes

Nutrition Information Per Serving (1 serving unit):

Calories: 280, Carbohydrates: 1g, Saturated Fat: 4g, Protein: 20g, Fat: 22g, Sodium: 480mg, Potassium: 160mg, Fiber: 0g, Sugar: 0g, Vitamin C: 5mg, Calcium: 20mg, Iron: 1mg.

Ingredients:

- 2 lbs chicken wings
- 2 tbsp olive oil
- 2 tbsp fresh lemon juice
- 2 tsp lemon zest
- 3 cloves garlic, minced
- 1 tsp garlic powder
- 1 tsp smoked paprika
- 1/2 tsp black pepper
- 1/2 tsp salt
- Fresh parsley for garnish (optional)

Directions:

1. Preheat your air fryer to 375°F.
2. In a large bowl, toss the chicken wings with olive oil, lemon juice, lemon zest, minced garlic, garlic powder, smoked paprika, salt, and black pepper until evenly coated.
3. Arrange the wings in a single layer in the air fryer basket, ensuring they do not overlap.
4. Air fry for 22-25 minutes, flipping halfway through, until the wings are crispy and golden brown.
5. Remove the wings from the air fryer and let them rest for a couple of minutes.
6. Garnish with fresh parsley if desired and serve hot for a zesty, garlic-infused, keto-friendly poultry dish.

Buffalo Chicken Bites

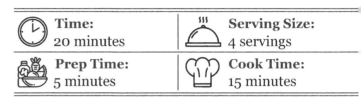

🕐 Time: 20 minutes	🍽 Serving Size: 4 servings
🥗 Prep Time: 5 minutes	👨‍🍳 Cook Time: 15 minutes

Nutrition Information Per Serving (1 serving):

Calories: 220, Carbohydrates: 2g, Saturated Fat: 5g, Protein: 26g, Fat: 12g, Sodium: 650mg, Potassium: 280mg, Fiber: 0g, Sugar: 1g, Vitamin C: 1mg, Calcium: 30mg, Iron: 1mg.

Ingredients:

- 1 lb boneless, skinless chicken breast, cut into bite-sized pieces
- 1/4 cup almond flour
- 1/4 cup grated Parmesan cheese
- 1 tsp garlic powder
- 1 tsp paprika
- Salt and black pepper to taste
- 2 tbsp unsalted butter, melted
- 1/4 cup buffalo sauce
- Olive oil spray
- Fresh celery sticks and ranch dressing (optional, for serving)

Directions:

1. Preheat your air fryer to 375°F.
2. In a small bowl, mix the almond flour, Parmesan cheese, garlic powder, paprika, salt, and black pepper.
3. Coat the chicken pieces in the almond flour mixture, ensuring they are fully covered.
4. Lightly spray the air fryer basket with olive oil and place the coated chicken bites in a single layer.
5. Air fry for 12-15 minutes, flipping halfway through, until the chicken bites are golden brown and cooked through.
6. In a separate bowl, mix the melted butter and buffalo sauce. Toss the cooked chicken bites in the buffalo sauce until fully coated.
7. Serve hot with fresh celery sticks and ranch dressing for a classic, keto-friendly buffalo chicken snack.

Air-Fried Chicken Cordon Bleu

🕐	Time: 25 minutes	🍲	Serving Size: 2 servings
🥗	Prep Time: 10 minutes	👨‍🍳	Cook Time: 15 minutes

Nutrition Information Per Serving (1 chicken breast):

Calories: 380, Carbohydrates: 4g, Saturated Fat: 8g, Protein: 42g, Fat: 20g, Sodium: 700mg, Potassium: 450mg, Fiber: 1g, Sugar: 1g, Vitamin C: 2mg, Calcium: 150mg, Iron: 1.5mg.

Ingredients:

- 2 boneless, skinless chicken breasts
- 2 slices Swiss cheese
- 2 slices ham
- 1/4 cup almond flour
- 1/4 cup grated Parmesan cheese
- 1 tsp garlic powder
- 1/2 tsp smoked paprika
- 1 large egg, beaten
- Salt and black pepper to taste
- Olive oil spray

Directions:

1. Preheat your air fryer to 375°F.
2. Butterfly each chicken breast by slicing it horizontally, being careful not to cut all the way through. Open the breast like a book and place one slice of ham and one slice of Swiss cheese inside each. Fold the chicken breasts back over to enclose the fillings.
3. In a small bowl, mix the almond flour, Parmesan cheese, garlic powder, smoked paprika, salt, and black pepper.
4. Dip each stuffed chicken breast into the beaten egg, then coat it in the almond flour mixture, pressing the coating onto the chicken.
5. Lightly spray the air fryer basket with olive oil and place the chicken breasts in a single layer.
6. Air fry for 12-15 minutes, flipping halfway through, until the chicken is golden and cooked through (internal temperature of 165°F).
7. Remove the chicken from the air fryer and let it rest for a few minutes before serving. Enjoy this keto-friendly take on Chicken Cordon Bleu with a crispy, flavorful coating.

Sesame Ginger Chicken Skewers

🕐	Time: 25 minutes	🍲	Serving Size: 4 skewers
🥗	Prep Time: 10 minutes	👨‍🍳	Cook Time: 15 minutes

Nutrition Information Per Serving (1 skewer):

Calories: 180, Carbohydrates: 2g, Saturated Fat: 2g, Protein: 25g, Fat: 8g, Sodium: 420mg, Potassium: 350mg, Fiber: 0g, Sugar: 1g, Vitamin C: 2mg, Calcium: 40mg, Iron: 1mg.

Ingredients:

- 1 lb boneless, skinless chicken breast, cut into bite-sized cubes
- 2 tbsp sesame oil
- 1 tbsp fresh ginger, grated
- 1 tbsp soy sauce (or tamari for gluten-free)
- 1 tbsp rice vinegar
- 1 tsp garlic powder
- 1 tsp sesame seeds
- 1/4 tsp red pepper flakes (optional)
- Salt and black pepper to taste
- Wooden skewers, soaked in water

Directions:

1. Preheat your air fryer to 375°F.
2. In a bowl, whisk together the sesame oil, grated ginger, soy sauce, rice vinegar, garlic powder, sesame seeds, red pepper flakes (if using), salt, and black pepper.
3. Add the chicken cubes to the marinade and toss until well coated. Let it marinate for 10 minutes.
4. Thread the marinated chicken cubes onto the soaked wooden skewers.
5. Lightly spray the air fryer basket with olive oil and place the skewers in a single layer.
6. Air fry for 12-15 minutes, flipping halfway through, until the chicken is cooked through and golden brown.
7. Remove the skewers from the air fryer and let them cool for a couple of minutes before serving. Enjoy these sesame ginger chicken skewers as a flavorful, keto-friendly poultry dish.

Bacon-Wrapped Stuffed Chicken Breasts

🕐	**Time:** 30 minutes	🍽	**Serving Size:** 2 chicken breasts
🥗	**Prep Time:** 10 minutes	👨‍🍳	**Cook Time:** 20 minutes

Nutrition Information Per Serving (1 stuffed chicken breast):
Calories: 420, Carbohydrates: 2g, Saturated Fat: 8g, Protein: 45g, Fat: 25g, Sodium: 780mg, Potassium: 400mg, Fiber: 0g, Sugar: 0g, Vitamin C: 1mg, Calcium: 80mg, Iron: 1.5mg.

Ingredients:
- 2 boneless, skinless chicken breasts
- 4 slices of bacon
- 1/2 cup shredded mozzarella cheese
- 2 tbsp cream cheese, softened
- 1/4 cup chopped spinach (fresh or frozen, thawed and squeezed dry)
- 1 tsp garlic powder
- 1 tsp Italian seasoning
- Salt and black pepper to taste
- Olive oil spray

Directions:
1. Preheat your air fryer to 375°F.
2. Butterfly the chicken breasts by slicing them horizontally but not all the way through, then open them like a book. Season with garlic powder, Italian seasoning, salt, and black pepper.
3. In a small bowl, mix together the shredded mozzarella, cream cheese, and chopped spinach. Spread the mixture evenly inside each chicken breast and fold the breast back over to seal.
4. Wrap two slices of bacon around each stuffed chicken breast, securing them with toothpicks if necessary.
5. Lightly spray the air fryer basket with olive oil and place the stuffed chicken breasts in a single layer.
6. Air fry for 18-20 minutes, flipping halfway through, until the bacon is crispy and the chicken reaches an internal temperature of 165°F.
7. Remove the chicken from the air fryer, let it rest for a few minutes, and then serve hot. Enjoy these juicy, bacon-wrapped stuffed chicken breasts as a keto-friendly, protein-packed dish!

Keto Chicken Fajita Bowls

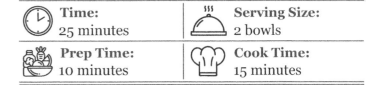

🕐	**Time:** 25 minutes	🍽	**Serving Size:** 2 bowls
🥗	**Prep Time:** 10 minutes	👨‍🍳	**Cook Time:** 15 minutes

Nutrition Information Per Serving (1 bowl):
Calories: 320, Carbohydrates: 6g, Saturated Fat: 6g, Protein: 32g, Fat: 18g, Sodium: 680mg, Potassium: 450mg, Fiber: 3g, Sugar: 2g, Vitamin C: 35mg, Calcium: 120mg, Iron: 1.5mg.

Ingredients:
- 2 boneless, skinless chicken breasts, sliced into strips
- 1 bell pepper, sliced (any color)
- 1/2 red onion, sliced
- 1 tbsp olive oil
- 1 tsp chili powder
- 1/2 tsp cumin
- 1/2 tsp garlic powder
- 1/2 tsp smoked paprika
- Salt and black pepper to taste
- 1/2 cup shredded cheddar cheese
- 1/2 avocado, sliced
- 2 tbsp sour cream (optional)
- Fresh cilantro for garnish

Directions:
1. Preheat your air fryer to 375°F.
2. In a bowl, toss the chicken strips with olive oil, chili powder, cumin, garlic powder, smoked paprika, salt, and black pepper until well coated.
3. Place the seasoned chicken, bell pepper, and red onion in the air fryer basket in a single layer.
4. Air fry for 12-15 minutes, flipping halfway through, until the chicken is cooked through and the vegetables are tender.
5. Once cooked, divide the chicken and vegetables between two bowls.
6. Top each bowl with shredded cheddar cheese, avocado slices, and a dollop of sour cream, if using.
7. Garnish with fresh cilantro and serve immediately for a flavorful, keto-friendly fajita bowl.

Air-Fried Chicken Meatballs

Time: 20 minutes	Serving Size: 4 servings
Prep Time: 10 minutes	Cook Time: 10 minutes

Nutrition Information Per Serving (1 serving of 3 meatballs):

Calories: 210, Carbohydrates: 2g, Saturated Fat: 3g, Protein: 24g, Fat: 12g, Sodium: 450mg, Potassium: 300mg, Fiber: 1g, Sugar: 0g, Vitamin C: 0mg, Calcium: 50mg, Iron: 1mg.

Ingredients:

- 1 lb ground chicken
- 1/4 cup almond flour
- 1/4 cup grated Parmesan cheese
- 1 large egg
- 2 tbsp fresh parsley, chopped
- 1 tsp garlic powder
- 1/2 tsp onion powder
- 1/2 tsp smoked paprika
- 1/4 tsp salt
- 1/4 tsp black pepper
- Olive oil spray

Directions:

1. Preheat your air fryer to 375°F.
2. In a large bowl, combine the ground chicken, almond flour, Parmesan cheese, egg, parsley, garlic powder, onion powder, smoked paprika, salt, and black pepper. Mix until all ingredients are well incorporated.
3. Form the mixture into 12 evenly-sized meatballs.
4. Lightly spray the air fryer basket with olive oil and place the meatballs in a single layer, ensuring they do not touch.
5. Air fry for 10 minutes, flipping halfway through, until the meatballs are golden brown and cooked through (internal temperature of 165°F).
6. Remove from the air fryer and serve hot. Enjoy these protein-packed, keto-friendly chicken meatballs as a main dish or snack!

Cajun Chicken Tenders

Time: 20 minutes	Serving Size: 4 servings
Prep Time: 5 minutes	Cook Time: 15 minutes

Nutrition Information Per Serving (1 serving):

Calories: 220, Carbohydrates: 3g, Saturated Fat: 2g, Protein: 28g, Fat: 10g, Sodium: 600mg, Potassium: 420mg, Fiber: 1g, Sugar: 1g, Vitamin C: 2mg, Calcium: 30mg, Iron: 1mg.

Ingredients:

- 1 lb chicken tenders
- 2 tbsp olive oil
- 1/4 cup almond flour
- 1/4 cup grated Parmesan cheese
- 1 tbsp Cajun seasoning
- 1/2 tsp garlic powder
- 1/4 tsp smoked paprika
- Salt and black pepper to taste
- Olive oil spray

Directions:

1. Preheat your air fryer to 375°F.
2. In a small bowl, combine the almond flour, Parmesan cheese, Cajun seasoning, garlic powder, smoked paprika, salt, and black pepper.
3. Coat the chicken tenders with olive oil, then dredge each tender in the almond flour mixture, ensuring an even coating.
4. Lightly spray the air fryer basket with olive oil and place the chicken tenders in a single layer.
5. Air fry for 12-15 minutes, flipping halfway through, until the chicken is golden brown and cooked through (internal temperature of 165°F).
6. Remove the chicken tenders from the air fryer and serve hot. These spicy, keto-friendly Cajun chicken tenders are perfect as a main dish or snack!

Keto Chicken Florentine

Time: 25 minutes	Serving Size: 2 stuffed chicken
Prep Time: 5 minutes	Cook Time: 20 minutes

Nutrition Information Per Serving (1 stuffed chicken breast):

Calories: 340, Carbohydrates: 4g, Saturated Fat: 7g, Protein: 36g, Fat: 20g, Sodium: 500mg, Potassium: 480mg, Fiber: 1g, Sugar: 1g, Vitamin C: 5mg, Calcium: 150mg, Iron: 1.5mg.

Ingredients:

- 2 boneless, skinless chicken breasts
- 2 tbsp olive oil
- 1/2 cup fresh spinach, chopped
- 1/4 cup heavy cream
- 1/4 cup shredded mozzarella cheese
- 1/4 cup grated Parmesan cheese
- 1 clove garlic, minced
- 1 tsp Italian seasoning
- Salt and black pepper to taste
- Olive oil spray

Directions:

1. Preheat your air fryer to 375°F.
2. Season the chicken breasts with salt, black pepper, and Italian seasoning. Lightly spray the air fryer basket with olive oil and place the chicken breasts in a single layer.
3. Air fry for 12-15 minutes, flipping halfway through, until the chicken is cooked through and reaches an internal temperature of 165°F.
4. While the chicken is cooking, heat olive oil in a small pan over medium heat. Add minced garlic and sauté for 1 minute until fragrant.
5. Stir in the chopped spinach and cook until wilted. Pour in the heavy cream, and add the mozzarella and Parmesan cheese. Stir until the cheese is melted and the sauce is creamy.
6. Once the chicken is cooked, spoon the creamy spinach mixture over the chicken breasts.
7. Return the chicken to the air fryer and cook for an additional 2-3 minutes, allowing the sauce to meld with the chicken.
8. Serve hot for a flavorful, keto-friendly Chicken Florentine dish.

Mediterranean Stuffed Chicken

Time: 30 minutes	Serving Size: 2 stuffed chicken
Prep Time: 10 minutes	Cook Time: 20 minutes

Nutrition Information Per Serving (1 stuffed chicken breast):

Calories: 320, Carbohydrates: 3g, Saturated Fat: 8g, Protein: 35g, Fat: 18g, Sodium: 650mg, Potassium: 450mg, Fiber: 1g, Sugar: 1g, Vitamin C: 6mg, Calcium: 100mg, Iron: 1.5m g.

Ingredients:

- 2 boneless, skinless chicken breasts
- 1/4 cup crumbled feta cheese
- 1/4 cup chopped spinach (fresh or thawed frozen)
- 2 tbsp sun-dried tomatoes, chopped
- 1 tbsp black olives, chopped
- 1 tbsp olive oil
- 1 tsp dried oregano
- 1 clove garlic, minced
- Salt and black pepper to taste
- Olive oil spray

Directions:

1. Preheat your air fryer to 375°F.
2. Butterfly each chicken breast by slicing them horizontally but not all the way through. Open the chicken breasts like a book.
3. In a small bowl, combine the feta cheese, spinach, sun-dried tomatoes, black olives, garlic, oregano, salt, and black pepper.
4. Spoon the filling mixture into the center of each chicken breast, then fold the chicken over to enclose the filling. Secure with toothpicks if necessary.
5. Lightly spray the air fryer basket with olive oil and place the stuffed chicken breasts in a single layer.
6. Brush the chicken with olive oil and air fry for 18-20 minutes, flipping halfway through, until the chicken is golden and cooked through (internal temperature of 165°F).
7. Remove the chicken from the air fryer and let it rest for a few minutes. Serve hot for a Mediterranean-inspired, keto-friendly dish packed with flavor!

Spicy Air-Fried Chicken Nuggets

 Time: 20 minutes	Serving Size: 4 servings
Prep Time: 5 minutes	Cook Time: 15 minutes

Nutrition Information Per Serving (1 serving unit):

Calories: 230, Carbohydrates: 3g, Saturated Fat: 3g, Protein: 25g, Fat: 13g, Sodium: 550mg, Potassium: 400mg, Fiber: 1g, Sugar: 0g, Vitamin C: 2mg, Calcium: 30mg, Iron: 1mg.

Ingredients:

- 1 lb boneless, skinless chicken breasts, cut into bite-sized pieces
- 1/4 cup almond flour
- 1/4 cup grated Parmesan cheese
- 1 large egg
- 1 tbsp hot sauce
- 1 tsp cayenne pepper (adjust to taste)
- 1/2 tsp garlic powder
- 1/2 tsp paprika
- Salt and black pepper to taste
- Olive oil spray

Directions:

1. Preheat your air fryer to 375°F.
2. In a small bowl, whisk the egg and hot sauce together. In another bowl, combine the almond flour, Parmesan cheese, cayenne pepper, garlic powder, paprika, salt, and black pepper.
3. Dip each chicken piece into the egg mixture, then coat it in the almond flour mixture, ensuring an even layer.
4. Lightly spray the air fryer basket with olive oil and arrange the coated chicken pieces in a single layer.
5. Air fry for 12-15 minutes, flipping halfway through, until the chicken nuggets are crispy and golden brown.
6. Serve hot with your favorite keto-friendly dipping sauce for a spicy, crunchy, and protein-packed snack or meal!

Rosemary and Garlic Chicken Thighs

Time: 30 minutes	Serving Size: 4 chicken thighs
Prep Time: 5 minutes	Cook Time: 25 minutes

Nutrition Information Per Serving (1 chicken thigh):

Calories: 300, Carbohydrates: 2g, Saturated Fat: 6g, Protein: 30g, Fat: 20g, Sodium: 400mg, Potassium: 320mg, Fiber: 1g, Sugar: 0g, Vitamin C: 1mg, Calcium: 20mg, Iron: 1.5mg.

Ingredients:

- 4 bone-in, skin-on chicken thighs
- 2 tbsp olive oil
- 2 tsp fresh rosemary, chopped
- 4 cloves garlic, minced
- 1 tsp garlic powder
- 1 tsp onion powder
- 1 tsp smoked paprika
- Salt and black pepper to taste
- Olive oil spray

Directions:

1. Preheat your air fryer to 375°F.
2. In a small bowl, mix the olive oil, chopped rosemary, minced garlic, garlic powder, onion powder, smoked paprika, salt, and black pepper to create a marinade.
3. Rub the marinade evenly over the chicken thighs, making sure to coat both the skin and the meat.
4. Lightly spray the air fryer basket with olive oil and place the chicken thighs skin-side up in a single layer.
5. Air fry for 22-25 minutes, flipping halfway through, until the skin is crispy and the chicken reaches an internal temperature of 165°F.
6. Remove the chicken thighs from the air fryer and let them rest for a few minutes before serving. Enjoy these flavorful, keto-friendly rosemary and garlic chicken thighs for a delicious and easy meal!

Chapter 5: Beef, Pork, and Lamb

Garlic Butter Ribeye Steaks

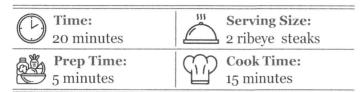

	Time: 20 minutes		Serving Size: 2 ribeye steaks
	Prep Time: 5 minutes		Cook Time: 15 minutes

Nutrition Information Per Serving (1 ribeye steak):

Calories: 450, Carbohydrates: 2g, Saturated Fat: 18g, Protein: 35g, Fat: 35g, Sodium: 320mg, Potassium: 450mg, Fiber: 0g, Sugar: 0g, Vitamin C: 0mg, Calcium: 30mg, Iron: 3mg.

Ingredients:

- 2 ribeye steaks (about 1 inch thick)
- 2 tbsp unsalted butter, softened
- 3 cloves garlic, minced
- 1 tsp fresh rosemary, chopped
- 1 tsp fresh thyme, chopped
- Salt and black pepper to taste
- Olive oil spray

Directions:

1. Preheat your air fryer to 400°F.
2. Pat the ribeye steaks dry with a paper towel and season generously with salt and black pepper on both sides.
3. In a small bowl, mix together the softened butter, minced garlic, rosemary, and thyme until well combined.
4. Lightly spray the air fryer basket with olive oil and place the steaks in a single layer.
5. Air fry for 10-12 minutes, flipping halfway through, until the steaks reach your desired doneness (135°F for medium-rare).
6. Once cooked, remove the steaks from the air fryer and immediately top each one with the garlic herb butter. Let the steaks rest for 5 minutes, allowing the butter to melt over the top.
7. Serve hot for a juicy and flavorful keto-friendly steak dinner.

Air-Fried Bacon-Wrapped Meatloaf

 Time:
40 minutes

 Serving Size:
4 slices

 Prep Time:
10 minutes

 Cook Time:
30 minutes

Nutrition Information Per Serving (1 slice):
Calories: 400, Carbohydrates: 3g, Saturated Fat: 12g, Protein: 35g, Fat: 28g, Sodium: 700mg, Potassium: 400mg, Fiber: 1g, Sugar: 1g, Vitamin C: 0mg, Calcium: 80mg, Iron: 2.5mg.

Ingredients:

- 1 lb ground beef
- 1/4 cup almond flour
- 1/4 cup grated Parmesan cheese
- 1 large egg
- 1 small onion, finely chopped
- 2 cloves garlic, minced
- 1 tbsp tomato paste
- (or sugar-free ketchup)
- 1 tsp Worcestershire sauce
- 1 tsp smoked paprika
- 1 tsp dried oregano
- Salt and black pepper to taste
- 6-8 slices of bacon
- Olive oil spray

Directions:

1. Preheat your air fryer to 350°F.
2. In a large bowl, mix the ground beef, almond flour, Parmesan cheese, egg, chopped onion, minced garlic, tomato paste, Worcestershire sauce, smoked paprika, oregano, salt, and black pepper until well combined.
3. Shape the mixture into a loaf and wrap it with the bacon slices, ensuring the ends of the bacon are tucked under the loaf to hold them in place.
4. Lightly spray the air fryer basket with olive oil and place the meatloaf in the basket.
5. Air fry for 25-30 minutes, or until the bacon is crispy and the internal temperature of the meatloaf reaches 160°F.
6. Remove the meatloaf from the air fryer and let it rest for 5 minutes before slicing. Serve hot for a hearty and keto-friendly meal packed with flavor.

Keto Pork Rind-Crusted Pork Chops

 Time:
20 minutes

 Serving Size:
2 pork chops

 Prep Time:
5 minutes

 Cook Time:
15 minutes

Nutrition Information Per Serving (1 pork chop):
Calories: 340, Carbohydrates: 1g, Saturated Fat: 6g, Protein: 36g, Fat: 20g, Sodium: 600mg, Potassium: 450mg, Fiber: 0g, Sugar: 0g, Vitamin C: 0mg, Calcium: 30mg, Iron: 1.2mg.

Ingredients:

- 2 boneless pork chops (about 1 inch thick)
- 1 cup crushed pork rinds
- 1/4 cup grated Parmesan cheese
- 1 tsp garlic powder
- 1/2 tsp smoked paprika
- 1 large egg
- Salt and black pepper to taste
- Olive oil spray

Directions:

1. Preheat your air fryer to 375°F.
2. In a bowl, combine the crushed pork rinds, Parmesan cheese, garlic powder, smoked paprika, salt, and black pepper.
3. In another small bowl, whisk the egg.
4. Dip each pork chop into the egg mixture, then coat it evenly with the pork rind mixture, pressing gently to ensure the coating sticks.
5. Lightly spray the air fryer basket with olive oil and place the pork chops in a single layer.
6. Air fry for 12-15 minutes, flipping halfway through, until the pork chops are golden brown and reach an internal temperature of 145°F.
7. Remove from the air fryer and let the pork chops rest for a few minutes before serving. Enjoy these crispy, keto-friendly pork chops for a satisfying and flavorful meal!

Rosemary Lamb Chops

Time: 20 minutes	Serving Size: 4 lamb chops
Prep Time: 5 minutes	Cook Time: 15 minutes

Nutrition Information Per Serving (1 lamb chop):

Calories: 380, Carbohydrates: 1g, Saturated Fat: 10g, Protein: 28g, Fat: 30g, Sodium: 400mg, Potassium: 320mg, Fiber: 0g, Sugar: 0g, Vitamin C: 0mg, Calcium: 20mg, Iron: 2mg.

Ingredients:

- 4 lamb chops (about 1 inch thick)
- 2 tbsp olive oil
- 2 tsp fresh rosemary, chopped
- 2 cloves garlic, minced
- 1 tsp lemon zest
- Salt and black pepper to taste
- Olive oil spray

Directions:

1. Preheat your air fryer to 400°F.
2. In a small bowl, mix the olive oil, chopped rosemary, minced garlic, lemon zest, salt, and black pepper to create a marinade.
3. Rub the marinade evenly over both sides of the lamb chops.
4. Lightly spray the air fryer basket with olive oil and place the lamb chops in a single layer.
5. Air fry for 10-12 minutes, flipping halfway through, until the lamb chops reach your desired level of doneness (145°F for medium-rare).
6. Remove the lamb chops from the air fryer and let them rest for a few minutes before serving. Enjoy these tender and flavorful keto-friendly rosemary lamb chops as a satisfying main course!

Keto Beef Kabobs

Time: 25 minutes	Serving Size: 4 skewers
Prep Time: 10 minutes	Cook Time: 15 minutes

Nutrition Information Per Serving (1 skewer):

Calories: 320, Carbohydrates: 3g, Saturated Fat: 6g, Protein: 28g, Fat: 21g, Sodium: 450mg, Potassium: 400mg, Fiber: 1g, Sugar: 1g, Vitamin C: 10mg, Calcium: 25mg, Iron: 3mg.

Ingredients:

- 1 lb beef sirloin, cut into 1-inch cubes
- 1 red bell pepper, cut into chunks
- 1 small zucchini, cut into thick slices
- 1 small red onion, cut into wedges
- 2 tbsp olive oil
- 1 tbsp lemon juice
- 1 tsp garlic powder
- 1 tsp smoked paprika
- 1/2 tsp dried oregano
- Salt and black pepper to taste
- Wooden skewers, soaked in water

Directions:

1. Preheat your air fryer to 375°F.
2. In a bowl, whisk together the olive oil, lemon juice, garlic powder, smoked paprika, oregano, salt, and black pepper.
3. Add the beef cubes to the marinade and toss to coat evenly. Let it marinate for 5 minutes.
4. Thread the beef, bell pepper, zucchini, and red onion alternately onto the soaked wooden skewers.
5. Lightly spray the air fryer basket with olive oil and place the skewers in a single layer.
6. Air fry for 12-15 minutes, flipping halfway through, until the beef is cooked to your desired doneness (135°F for medium-rare).
7. Remove from the air fryer and let the kabobs rest for a few minutes before serving. Enjoy these flavorful, keto-friendly beef kabobs for a hearty meal!

Air-Fried Pork Belly Bites

 Time:
25 minutes

 Serving Size:
4 serving bowls

 Prep Time:
5 minutes

 Cook Time:
20 minutes

Nutrition Information Per Serving (1 serving bowl):

Calories: 450, Carbohydrates: 1g, Saturated Fat: 16g, Protein: 15g, Fat: 40g, Sodium: 800mg, Potassium: 200mg, Fiber: 0g, Sugar: 0g, Vitamin C: 0mg, Calcium: 20mg, Iron: 1mg.

Ingredients:

- 1 lb pork belly, cut into 1-inch cubes
- 1 tsp garlic powder
- 1 tsp smoked paprika
- 1/2 tsp onion powder
- 1/2 tsp salt
- 1/4 tsp black pepper
- Olive oil spray

Directions:

1. Preheat your air fryer to 400°F.
2. In a small bowl, combine the garlic powder, smoked paprika, onion powder, salt, and black pepper.
3. Toss the pork belly cubes in the spice mixture until evenly coated.
4. Lightly spray the air fryer basket with olive oil and place the pork belly cubes in a single layer.
5. Air fry for 18-20 minutes, shaking the basket halfway through, until the pork belly is crispy and golden brown.
6. Remove from the air fryer and let the pork belly bites rest for a few minutes before serving. Enjoy these savory, keto-friendly pork belly bites as a snack or appetizer!

Herb-Crusted Rack of Lamb

 Time:
30 minutes

 Serving Size:
4 servings

 Prep Time:
10 minutes

Cook Time:
20 minutes

Nutrition Information Per Serving (1 serving unit):

Calories: 420, Carbohydrates: 2g, Saturated Fat: 14g, Protein: 30g, Fat: 34g, Sodium: 400mg, Potassium: 350mg, Fiber: 0g, Sugar: 0g, Vitamin C: 2mg, Calcium: 40mg, Iron: 3mg.

Ingredients:

- 1 rack of lamb (about 1-1.5 lbs)
- 2 tbsp olive oil
- 2 cloves garlic, minced
- 2 tbsp fresh rosemary, chopped
- 1 tbsp fresh thyme, chopped
- 1 tsp Dijon mustard
- 1/2 tsp salt
- 1/4 tsp black pepper
- Olive oil spray

Directions:

1. Preheat your air fryer to 375°F.
2. In a small bowl, mix together the olive oil, minced garlic, chopped rosemary, thyme, Dijon mustard, salt, and black pepper to form a paste.
3. Rub the herb mixture evenly over the entire rack of lamb.
4. Lightly spray the air fryer basket with olive oil and place the rack of lamb, fat side up, in the basket.
5. Air fry for 18-20 minutes, flipping halfway through, until the internal temperature reaches 135°F for medium-rare.
6. Remove the lamb from the air fryer and let it rest for 5 minutes before slicing into individual chops.
7. Serve hot for a flavorful and elegant keto-friendly meal!

Spicy Beef Empanadas

 Time: 30 minutes

 Serving Size: 4 empanadas

 Prep Time: 10 minutes

 Cook Time: 20 minutes

Nutrition Information Per Serving (1 empanada):

Calories: 350, Carbohydrates: 5g, Saturated Fat: 9g, Protein: 24g, Fat: 28g, Sodium: 520mg, Potassium: 320mg, Fiber: 2g, Sugar: 1g, Vitamin C: 3mg, Calcium: 50mg, Iron: 3mg.

Ingredients:

- 1/2 lb ground beef
- 1/2 small onion, finely chopped
- 2 cloves garlic, minced
- 1/2 tsp smoked paprika
- 1/2 tsp cumin
- 1/4 tsp cayenne pepper (adjust to taste)
- Salt and black pepper to taste
- 1/4 cup shredded cheddar cheese
- 1/4 cup almond flour
- 2 tbsp coconut flour
- 1 large egg
- 2 tbsp butter, melted
- 2 tbsp water
- Olive oil spray

Directions:

1. Preheat your air fryer to 375°F.
2. In a skillet, cook the ground beef over medium heat until browned. Add the chopped onion, minced garlic, smoked paprika, cumin, cayenne pepper, salt, and black pepper. Cook for another 5 minutes until the onion softens. Stir in the shredded cheddar cheese and remove from heat. Set aside.
3. In a bowl, combine the almond flour, coconut flour, melted butter, and water. Mix until a dough forms. Divide into 4 equal parts and flatten each part into a circle.
4. Spoon the beef mixture in the center of each dough circle. Fold the dough over to form a half-moon shape and press the edges together to seal. Use a fork to crimp the edges.
5. Lightly spray the air fryer basket with olive oil and place the empanadas in a single layer.
6. Air fry for 10-12 minutes, flipping halfway through, until golden brown and crispy.
7. Remove from the air fryer, let cool, and enjoy these spicy, keto-friendly beef empanadas!

Keto BBQ Pulled Pork

 Time: 45 minutes

 Serving Size: 4 serving plates

 Prep Time: 5 minutes

 Cook Time: 40 minutes

Nutrition Information Per Serving (1 serving plate):

Calories: 380, Carbohydrates: 4g, Saturated Fat: 10g, Protein: 28g, Fat: 28g, Sodium: 700mg, Potassium: 400mg, Fiber: 1g, Sugar: 1g, Vitamin C: 0mg, Calcium: 30mg, Iron: 2mg.

Ingredients:

- 1 lb pork shoulder, cut into chunks
- 1/4 cup sugar-free BBQ sauce
- 1 tbsp smoked paprika
- 1 tsp garlic powder
- 1 tsp onion powder
- 1/2 tsp ground cumin
- 1/2 tsp black pepper
- 1/2 tsp salt
- Olive oil spray

Directions:

1. Preheat your air fryer to 375°F.
2. In a small bowl, mix the smoked paprika, garlic powder, onion powder, cumin, black pepper, and salt.
3. Rub the spice mixture all over the pork shoulder chunks.
4. Lightly spray the air fryer basket with olive oil and place the pork chunks in a single layer.
5. Air fry for 35-40 minutes, flipping halfway through, until the pork is tender and has an internal temperature of 190°F.
6. Remove the pork from the air fryer and let it rest for 5 minutes. Shred the pork using two forks.
7. Toss the shredded pork with the sugar-free BBQ sauce.
8. Serve hot, either on its own or as a filling for keto-friendly buns, for a delicious, low-carb BBQ pulled pork dish!

Crispy Pork Schnitzel

Time: 25 minutes	Serving Size: 2 pork chops
Prep Time: 10 minutes	Cook Time: 15 minutes

Nutrition Information Per Serving (1 schnitzel):

Calories: 420, Carbohydrates: 3g, Saturated Fat: 9g, Protein: 35g, Fat: 28g, Sodium: 550mg, Potassium: 450mg, Fiber: 1g, Sugar: 1g, Vitamin C: 0mg, Calcium: 60mg, Iron: 2mg.

Ingredients:

- 2 boneless pork chops (thinly pounded to 1/4 inch thickness)
- 1/2 cup almond flour
- 1/4 cup grated Parmesan cheese
- 1 large egg
- 1 tsp garlic powder
- 1/2 tsp smoked paprika
- Salt and black pepper to taste
- Olive oil spray
- Lemon wedges for serving

Directions:

1. Preheat your air fryer to 375°F.
2. In a shallow bowl, whisk the egg. In another shallow bowl, combine the almond flour, Parmesan cheese, garlic powder, smoked paprika, salt, and black pepper.
3. Dip each pork chop into the egg mixture, then dredge it in the almond flour mixture, ensuring the pork is evenly coated.
4. Lightly spray the air fryer basket with olive oil and place the breaded pork chops in a single layer.
5. Air fry for 12-15 minutes, flipping halfway through, until the pork schnitzel is golden brown and crispy.
6. Remove from the air fryer and let the schnitzel rest for a couple of minutes.
7. Serve hot with lemon wedges for a keto-friendly, crispy pork schnitzel meal.

Air-Fried Beef Ribs

Time: 50 minutes	Serving Size: 2 servings
Prep Time: 10 minutes	Cook Time: 40 minutes

Nutrition Information Per Serving (1 serving unit):

Calories: 520, Carbohydrates: 2g, Saturated Fat: 16g, Protein: 38g, Fat: 40g, Sodium: 650mg, Potassium: 500mg, Fiber: 0g, Sugar: 0g, Vitamin C: 0mg, Calcium: 30mg, Iron: 4mg.

Ingredients:

- 1 lb beef short ribs
- 2 tbsp olive oil
- 1 tbsp smoked paprika
- 1 tsp garlic powder
- 1 tsp onion powder
- 1/2 tsp ground cumin
- 1/2 tsp black pepper
- 1/2 tsp salt
- 1 tsp dried thyme
- Olive oil spray

Directions:

1. Preheat your air fryer to 375°F.
2. In a small bowl, mix together the olive oil, smoked paprika, garlic powder, onion powder, cumin, black pepper, salt, and thyme to create a rub.
3. Rub the spice mixture evenly over the beef ribs, ensuring all sides are coated.
4. Lightly spray the air fryer basket with olive oil and place the beef ribs in a single layer.
5. Air fry for 35-40 minutes, flipping halfway through, until the ribs are tender and have an internal temperature of 195°F.
6. Remove from the air fryer and let the beef ribs rest for 5 minutes before serving.
7. Serve hot for a flavorful, tender, and keto-friendly beef rib dish.

Keto Bacon Cheeseburger Sliders

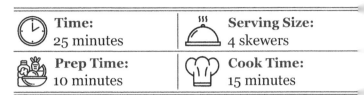 Time: 25 minutes	Serving Size: 4 sliders
Prep Time: 10 minutes	Cook Time: 15 minutes

Nutrition Information Per Serving (1 slider):

Calories: 320, Carbohydrates: 2g, Saturated Fat: 12g, Protein: 20g, Fat: 26g, Sodium: 650mg, Potassium: 320mg, Fiber: 0g, Sugar: 0g, Vitamin C: 0mg, Calcium: 100mg, Iron: 2mg.

Ingredients:
- 1 lb ground beef
- 4 slices of bacon, cooked and crumbled
- 1/2 cup shredded cheddar cheese
- 1 tsp garlic powder
- 1 tsp onion powder
- 1 tsp mustard
- Salt and black pepper to taste
- 4 large lettuce leaves (for wrapping)
- Pickle slices (optional)
- Olive oil spray

Directions:
1. Preheat your air fryer to 375°F.
2. In a bowl, combine the ground beef, crumbled bacon, shredded cheddar cheese, garlic powder, onion powder, mustard, salt, and black pepper. Mix until well combined.
3. Divide the mixture into 4 equal portions and shape them into small patties (sliders).
4. Lightly spray the air fryer basket with olive oil and place the patties in a single layer.
5. Air fry for 10-12 minutes, flipping halfway through, until the sliders are cooked through and reach an internal temperature of 160°F.
6. Remove from the air fryer and let the patties rest for a couple of minutes.
7. Serve the sliders wrapped in large lettuce leaves with optional pickle slices for a keto-friendly, low-carb bacon cheeseburger experience.

Beef and Broccoli Skewers

Time: 25 minutes	Serving Size: 4 skewers
Prep Time: 10 minutes	Cook Time: 15 minutes

Nutrition Information Per Serving (1 skewer):

Calories: 320, Carbohydrates: 4g, Saturated Fat: 8g, Protein: 28g, Fat: 22g, Sodium: 550mg, Potassium: 420mg, Fiber: 2g, Sugar: 1g, Vitamin C: 30mg, Calcium: 40mg, Iron: 3mg.

Ingredients:
- 1 lb beef sirloin, cut into bite-sized cubes
- 1 cup broccoli florets
- 1 tbsp olive oil
- 1 tbsp soy sauce (or coconut aminos for a lower-sodium option)
- 1 tsp garlic powder
- 1 tsp sesame oil
- 1/2 tsp ground ginger
- 1/4 tsp black pepper
- 1 tbsp sesame seeds (optional)
- Wooden skewers, soaked in water

Directions:
1. Preheat your air fryer to 375°F.
2. In a bowl, mix the olive oil, soy sauce, garlic powder, sesame oil, ground ginger, and black pepper to create a marinade.
3. Toss the beef cubes and broccoli florets in the marinade until well coated.
4. Thread the marinated beef and broccoli alternately onto the soaked wooden skewers.
5. Lightly spray the air fryer basket with olive oil and arrange the skewers in a single layer.
6. Air fry for 12-15 minutes, flipping halfway through, until the beef is cooked to your desired doneness (135°F for medium-rare) and the broccoli is tender.
7. Sprinkle sesame seeds over the skewers before serving, if desired. Enjoy these delicious, keto-friendly beef and broccoli skewers for a balanced, low-carb meal!

Italian Sausage-Stuffed Peppers

 Time:
30 minutes

 Serving Size:
2 stuffed bell peppers

 Prep Time:
10 minutes

 Cook Time:
20 minutes

Nutrition Information Per Serving (1 stuffed bell pepper):

Calories: 320, Carbohydrates: 7g, Saturated Fat: 8g, Protein: 24g, Fat: 22g, Sodium: 800mg, Potassium: 450mg, Fiber: 3g, Sugar: 3g, Vitamin C: 70mg, Calcium: 50mg, Iron: 2mg.

Ingredients:

- 2 large bell peppers, halved and seeded
- 1/2 lb Italian sausage (mild or hot, depending on preference)
- 1/4 cup shredded mozzarella cheese
- 1/4 cup grated Parmesan cheese
- 1/4 cup marinara sauce (sugar-free)
- 1 clove garlic, minced
- 1 tsp Italian seasoning
- 1/2 tsp smoked paprika
- Olive oil spray
- Fresh basil for garnish (optional)

Directions:

1. Preheat your air fryer to 360°F.
2. In a skillet over medium heat, cook the Italian sausage with minced garlic until browned, about 5 minutes. Drain any excess grease.
3. Add the marinara sauce, Italian seasoning, and smoked paprika to the sausage mixture. Stir to combine.
4. Stuff each bell pepper half with the sausage mixture, dividing it evenly.
5. Top each stuffed pepper with shredded mozzarella and Parmesan cheese.
6. Lightly spray the air fryer basket with olive oil and place the stuffed peppers in a single layer.
7. Air fry for 15-20 minutes, until the peppers are tender and the cheese is melted and bubbly.
8. Remove from the air fryer and garnish with fresh basil, if desired. Serve hot for a flavorful, keto-friendly stuffed pepper meal.

Crispy Keto Lamb Meatballs

 Time:
25 minutes

 Serving Size:
4 servings

 Prep Time:
10 minutes

 Cook Time:
15 minutes

Nutrition Information Per Serving (1 serving unit):

Calories: 320, Carbohydrates: 2g, Saturated Fat: 8g, Protein: 22g, Fat: 26g, Sodium: 450mg, Potassium: 300mg, Fiber: 1g, Sugar: 0g, Vitamin C: 1mg, Calcium: 40mg, Iron: 2mg.

Ingredients:

- 1 lb ground lamb
- 1/4 cup almond flour
- 1/4 cup grated Parmesan cheese
- 1 large egg
- 2 cloves garlic, minced
- 1 tbsp fresh parsley, chopped
- 1 tsp dried oregano
- 1/2 tsp ground cumin
- 1/4 tsp ground cinnamon
- Salt and black pepper to taste
- Olive oil spray

Directions:

1. Preheat your air fryer to 375°F.
2. In a large bowl, mix together the ground lamb, almond flour, Parmesan cheese, egg, minced garlic, parsley, oregano, cumin, cinnamon, salt, and black pepper until well combined.
3. Roll the mixture into small meatballs, about 1 inch in diameter, and set aside.
4. Lightly spray the air fryer basket with olive oil and place the meatballs in a single layer.
5. Air fry for 12-15 minutes, shaking the basket halfway through, until the meatballs are golden brown and crispy on the outside.
6. Remove from the air fryer and let the meatballs cool slightly before serving. Enjoy these flavorful, crispy keto lamb meatballs as a protein-packed appetizer or main dish!

Chapter 6: Fish and Seafood

Crispy Keto Fish Sticks

Time: 25 minutes	Serving Size: 2 plates
Prep Time: 10 minutes	Cook Time: 15 minutes

Nutrition Information Per Serving (1 white fish fillet):

Calories: 320, Carbohydrates: 3g, Saturated Fat: 5g, Protein: 25g, Fat: 22g, Sodium: 450mg, Potassium: 380mg, Fiber: 1g, Sugar: 0g, Vitamin C: 0mg, Calcium: 40mg, Iron: 1mg.

Ingredients:

- 2 white fish fillets (cod, haddock, or tilapia), cut into strips
- 1/2 cup almond flour
- 1/4 cup grated Parmesan cheese
- 1 large egg, beaten
- 1 tsp garlic powder
- 1 tsp smoked paprika
- 1/2 tsp dried thyme
- Salt and black pepper to taste
- Olive oil spray

Directions:

1. Preheat your air fryer to 375°F.
2. In a shallow bowl, mix together the almond flour, Parmesan cheese, garlic powder, smoked paprika, dried thyme, salt, and black pepper.
3. Make sure the fish is completely covered by dipping each strip of fish into the beaten egg and then dredging it in the almond flour mixture.
4. Arrange the fish sticks in a single layer inside the air fryer basket after giving it a quick spray of olive oil.
5. Air fry for 10-12 minutes, flipping halfway through, until the fish sticks are golden brown and crispy.
6. Remove from the air fryer and let them cool for a minute before serving. Enjoy these crispy, keto-friendly fish sticks with your favorite low-carb dipping sauce!

Cajun Shrimp Skewers

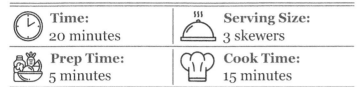 Time: 20 minutes	Serving Size: 3 skewers
Prep Time: 5 minutes	Cook Time: 15 minutes

Nutrition Information Per Serving (1 skewer):

Calories: 210, Carbohydrates: 2g, Saturated Fat: 3g, Protein: 28g, Fat: 10g, Sodium: 550mg, Potassium: 300mg, Fiber: 0g, Sugar: 1g, Vitamin C: 4mg, Calcium: 80mg, Iron: 2mg.

Ingredients:

- 1/2 lb large shrimp, peeled and deveined
- 1 tbsp olive oil
- 1 tbsp Cajun seasoning
- 1 tsp smoked paprika
- 1/2 tsp garlic powder
- 1/2 tsp onion powder
- 1/4 tsp cayenne pepper (optional for extra heat)
- Salt and black pepper to taste
- Lemon wedges for serving
- Wooden skewers, soaked in water

Directions:

1. Preheat your air fryer to 400°F.
2. In a bowl, toss the shrimp with olive oil, Cajun seasoning, smoked paprika, garlic powder, onion powder, cayenne pepper (if using), salt, and black pepper.
3. Thread the seasoned shrimp onto the soaked wooden skewers.
4. After giving the air fryer basket a quick spray of olive oil, place the skewers in a single layer.
5. Air fry for 8-10 minutes, flipping halfway through, until the shrimp are pink and cooked through.
6. Remove from the air fryer and serve with lemon wedges for a tangy finish. Enjoy these spicy, keto-friendly Cajun shrimp skewers as a perfect appetizer or main course!

Air-Fried Garlic Butter Lobster Tails

Time: 20 minutes	Serving Size: 2 lobster tails
Prep Time: 5 minutes	Cook Time: 15 minutes

Nutrition Information Per Serving (1 lobster tail):

Calories: 210, Carbohydrates: 1g, Saturated Fat: 8g, Protein: 25g, Fat: 14g, Sodium: 470mg, Potassium: 200mg, Fiber: 0g, Sugar: 0g, Vitamin C: 2mg, Calcium: 30mg, Iron: 1mg.

Ingredients:

- 2 lobster tails (about 5-6 oz each)
- 2 tbsp unsalted butter, melted
- 2 cloves garlic, minced
- 1 tbsp fresh parsley, chopped
- 1 tsp lemon juice
- Salt and black pepper to taste
- Lemon wedges for serving

Directions:

1. Preheat your air fryer to 380°F.
2. Cut a small lengthwise incision through the top of the lobster shells using kitchen scissors, then carefully remove the flesh, leaving it attached at the base. Position the meat above the shell.
3. Melted butter, minced garlic, parsley, lemon juice, salt, and black pepper should all be combined in a small bowl.
4. Drizzle the lobster meat with a large amount of the garlic butter mixture.
5. Pour a generous portion of the garlic butter mixture over the lobster meat.
6. Air fry for 8-10 minutes, until the lobster meat is opaque and cooked through, reaching an internal temperature of 145°F.
7. After taking the lobster tails out of the air fryer, serve them hot with lemon wedges for a decadent, keto-friendly seafood entrée.

Lemon Dill Salmon Fillets

 Time: 20 minutes

 Serving Size: 2 salomon fillets

 Prep Time: 5 minutes

 Cook Time: 15 minutes

Nutrition Information Per Serving (1 salmon fillet):

Calories: 280, Carbohydrates: 1g, Saturated Fat: 3g, Protein: 25g, Fat: 19g, Sodium: 350mg, Potassium: 700mg, Fiber: 0g, Sugar: 0g, Vitamin C: 3mg, Calcium: 30mg, Iron: 1mg.

Ingredients:

- 2 salmon fillets (about 6 oz each)
- 2 tbsp olive oil
- 1 tbsp fresh lemon juice
- 1 tbsp fresh dill, chopped
- 1 tsp lemon zest
- Salt and black pepper to taste
- Lemon wedges for serving

Directions:

1. Preheat your air fryer to 375°F.
2. Mix the olive oil, lemon juice, zest, chopped dill, salt, and black pepper in a small bowl.
3. Brush the salmon fillets with the lemon-dill mixture, coating both sides evenly.
4. After lightly misting the air fryer basket with olive oil, arrange the salmon fillets skin-side down in a single layer.
5. Air fry for 10-12 minutes, until the salmon is opaque and flakes easily with a fork, reaching an internal temperature of 145°F.
6. For a tasty, fresh, and keto-friendly seafood entrée, remove the salmon from the air fryer and serve it hot with lemon wedges.

Keto Coconut Shrimp

 Time: 20 minutes

 Serving Size: 2 servings

 Prep Time: 5 minutes

 Cook Time: 15 minutes

Nutrition Information Per Serving (1 serving unit):

Calories: 280, Carbohydrates: 4g, Saturated Fat: 9g, Protein: 23g, Fat: 18g, Sodium: 540mg, Potassium: 200mg, Fiber: 2g, Sugar: 1g, Vitamin C: 1mg, Calcium: 50mg, Iron: 1mg.

Ingredients:

- 12 large shrimp, peeled and deveined, tails on
- 1/2 cup unsweetened shredded coconut
- 1/4 cup almond flour
- 1 large egg, beaten
- 1 tsp garlic powder
- 1/2 tsp smoked paprika
- 1/4 tsp cayenne pepper (optional)
- Salt and black pepper to taste
- Olive oil spray
- Sugar-free dipping sauce (optional)

Directions:

1. Preheat your air fryer to 375°F.
2. In one bowl, mix the almond flour, garlic powder, smoked paprika, cayenne pepper (if using), salt, and black pepper. Put the egg into one bowl, the shredded coconut into another, and the beaten egg into a third.
3. Dip each shrimp first into the almond flour mixture, then into the egg, and finally coat with the shredded coconut. Press gently to ensure the coconut sticks well to the shrimp.
4. After giving the shrimp a little coating of olive oil, arrange them in a single layer within the air fryer basket.
5. The shrimp should be air-fried for 10–12 minutes, turning them halfway through, or until they are crispy and golden brown.
6. RThis is a tropical-inspired, keto-friendly dish that you can remove from the air fryer and serve hot with a sugar-free dipping sauce.

Air-Fried Crab Cakes

Time: 20 minutes	Serving Size: 4 crab cakes
Prep Time: 10 minutes	Cook Time: 10 minutes

Nutrition Information Per Serving (1 crab cake):

Calories: 220, Carbohydrates: 3g, Saturated Fat: 4g, Protein: 18g, Fat: 15g, Sodium: 520mg, Potassium: 180mg, Fiber: 1g, Sugar: 0g, Vitamin C: 2mg, Calcium: 40mg, Iron: 1mg.

Ingredients:

- 1 lb lump crab meat
- 1/4 cup almond flour
- 1 large egg, beaten
- 2 tbsp mayonnaise (sugar-free)
- 1 tbsp Dijon mustard
- 1 tsp lemon juice
- 1/2 tsp Old Bay seasoning
- 1/4 tsp garlic powder
- 2 tbsp fresh parsley, chopped
- Salt and black pepper to taste
- Olive oil spray
- Lemon wedges for serving

Directions:

1. Preheat your air fryer to 370°F.
2. In a large bowl, gently combine the crab meat, almond flour, beaten egg, mayonnaise, Dijon mustard, lemon juice, Old Bay seasoning, garlic powder, chopped parsley, salt, and black pepper.
3. Form the mixture into 4 evenly-sized crab cakes.
4. Spread a thin amount of olive oil into the air fryer basket, then add the crab cakes one at a time.
5. The crab cakes should air fried for 8 to 10 minutes, turning them halfway through, or until the outsides are crisp and golden brown.
6. Remove from the air fryer and serve with lemon wedges. Enjoy these keto-friendly, crispy crab cakes as an appetizer or light meal!

Spicy Tuna Patties

Time: 20 minutes	Serving Size: 4 tuna patties
Prep Time: 10 minutes	Cook Time: 10 minutes

Nutrition Information Per Serving (1 tuna patty):

Calories: 180, Carbohydrates: 2g, Saturated Fat: 3g, Protein: 22g, Fat: 10g, Sodium: 350mg, Potassium: 250mg, Fiber: 1g, Sugar: 0g, Vitamin C: 1mg, Calcium: 40mg, Iron: 1mg.

Ingredients:

- 2 cans tuna in water, drained
- 1/4 cup almond flour
- 1 large egg, beaten
- 1 tbsp mayonnaise (sugar-free)
- 1 tsp Dijon mustard
- 1 tsp Sriracha sauce (or to taste)
- 1/2 tsp garlic powder
- 1/2 tsp onion powder
- 1/4 tsp paprika
- Salt and black pepper to taste
- 2 tbsp fresh parsley, chopped
- Olive oil spray
- Lemon wedges for serving

Directions:

1. Preheat your air fryer to 375°F.
2. Tuna that has been drained and combined with almond flour, beaten egg, mayonnaise, Dijon mustard, Sriracha sauce, paprika, onion powder, garlic powder, salt, black pepper, and chopped parsley should all be combined in a big bowl.
3. Form the mixture into 4 patties.
4. Spread a thin amount of olive oil on the air fryer basket, then add the tuna patties one at a time.
5. Air fry for 8-10 minutes, flipping halfway through, until the patties are golden brown and crisp on the outside.
6. Remove from the air fryer and serve with lemon wedges. Enjoy these spicy, keto-friendly tuna patties as a satisfying meal or snack!

Parmesan-Crusted Cod

 Time:
20 minutes

 Serving Size:
4 cod fillets

 Prep Time:
5 minutes

 Cook Time:
15 minutes

Nutrition Information Per Serving (1 cod fillet):

Calories: 290, Carbohydrates: 3g, Saturated Fat: 5g, Protein: 32g, Fat: 16g, Sodium: 540mg, Potassium: 480mg, Fiber: 1g, Sugar: 0g, Vitamin C: 2mg, Calcium: 150mg, Iron: 1mg.

Ingredients:

- 2 cod fillets (about 6 oz each)
- 1/2 cup grated Parmesan cheese
- 1/4 cup almond flour
- 1 large egg, beaten
- 1 tsp garlic powder
- 1 tsp lemon zest
- 1/2 tsp smoked paprika
- Salt and black pepper to taste
- Olive oil spray
- Lemon wedges for serving

Directions:

1. Preheat your air fryer to 375°F.
2. In a shallow bowl, mix the Parmesan cheese, almond flour, garlic powder, lemon zest, smoked paprika, salt, and black pepper.
3. Dip each cod fillet into the beaten egg, then dredge it in the Parmesan mixture, pressing lightly to ensure an even coating.
4. Spread a thin amount of olive oil within the air fryer basket, then add the fillets one at a time.
5. Air fry for 12-15 minutes, flipping halfway through, until the cod is golden brown and flakes easily with a fork, reaching an internal temperature of 145°F.
6. Remove the cod from the air fryer and serve with lemon wedges for a fresh, tangy finish. Enjoy these crispy, keto-friendly Parmesan-crusted cod fillets!

Blackened Shrimp Lettuce Wraps

 Time:
20 minutes

 Serving Size:
2 wraps

 Prep Time:
5 minutes

 Cook Time:
15 minutes

Nutrition Information Per Serving (1 wrap):

Calories: 220, Carbohydrates: 3g, Saturated Fat: 4g, Protein: 28g, Fat: 12g, Sodium: 580mg, Potassium: 350mg, Fiber: 1g, Sugar: 1g, Vitamin C: 12mg, Calcium: 80mg, Iron: 2mg.

Ingredients:

- 12 large shrimp, peeled and deveined
- 1 tbsp olive oil
- 1 tbsp blackened seasoning (or Cajun seasoning)
- 1/2 tsp smoked paprika
- 1/4 tsp cayenne pepper (optional for extra heat)
- 1 tsp lemon juice
- Salt and black pepper to taste
- 4 large romaine lettuce leaves (or butter lettuce)
- 1/4 cup diced avocado
- 1/4 cup diced tomatoes
- 2 tbsp sour cream (optional)
- Lemon wedges for serving

Directions:

1. Preheat your air fryer to 375°F.
2. In a bowl, toss the shrimp with olive oil, blackened seasoning, smoked paprika, cayenne pepper (if using), lemon juice, salt, and black pepper until evenly coated.
3. After giving the air fryer basket a quick spray of olive oil, arrange the shrimp in a single layer.
4. Air fry for 8-10 minutes, flipping halfway through, until the shrimp are opaque and cooked through.
5. Assemble the lettuce wraps by placing shrimp in each lettuce leaf, and topping with diced avocado, tomatoes, and a dollop of sour cream, if desired.
6. Serve immediately with lemon wedges for a fresh, keto-friendly wrap bursting with flavor!

Keto Fish Tacos (Cabbage Shells)

Time: 25 minutes	Serving Size: 2 tacos
Prep Time: 10 minutes	Cook Time: 15 minutes

Nutrition Information Per Serving (1 taco):

Calories: 230, Carbohydrates: 4g, Saturated Fat: 5g, Protein: 24g, Fat: 15g, Sodium: 400mg, Potassium: 550mg, Fiber: 2g, Sugar: 1g, Vitamin C: 25mg, Calcium: 60mg, Iron: 1mg.

Ingredients:

- 2 white fish fillets (cod, tilapia, or haddock)
- 1/4 cup almond flour
- 1/4 cup grated Parmesan cheese
- 1 large egg, beaten
- 1 tsp smoked paprika
- 1/2 tsp garlic powder
- Salt and black pepper to taste
- 4 large cabbage leaves (for taco shells)
- 1/4 cup diced avocado
- 1/4 cup diced tomatoes
- 2 tbsp sour cream (optional)
- Fresh lime wedges for serving

Directions:

1. Preheat your air fryer to 375°F.
2. Combine the almond flour, Parmesan cheese, garlic powder, smoked paprika, salt, and black pepper in a small bowl.
3. After dipping each fish fillet into the beaten egg, coat it completely by dredging it in the almond flour mixture.
4. Fish fillets should be arranged in a single layer in the air fryer basket after lightly misting it with olive oil.
5. The fish should be air-fried for 10 to 12 minutes, turning it halfway through, or until it becomes golden and flake readily with a fork.
6. While the fish is cooking, gently steam the cabbage leaves until they are soft enough to fold, about 2 minutes.
7. Once the fish is cooked, break it into chunks and divide evenly between the cabbage leaves.
8. Top each taco with diced avocado, tomatoes, and a dollop of sour cream if desired. This taco will taste zesty and be keto-friendly when served with fresh lime wedges!

Herb Butter Scallops

Time: 15 minutes	Serving Size: 2 servings
Prep Time: 5 minutes	Cook Time: 10 minutes

Nutrition Information Per Serving (1 serving unit):

Calories: 220, Carbohydrates: 2g, Saturated Fat: 8g, Protein: 22g, Fat: 14g, Sodium: 570mg, Potassium: 320mg, Fiber: 0g, Sugar: 0g, Vitamin C: 1mg, Calcium: 12mg, Iron: 0.6mg.

Ingredients:

- 8 large sea scallops
- 2 tbsp unsalted butter, melted
- 1 tbsp fresh parsley, chopped
- 1 clove garlic, minced
- 1 tsp lemon zest
- Salt and black pepper to taste
- Olive oil spray
- Lemon wedges for serving

Directions:

1. Preheat your air fryer to 400°F.
2. After using paper towels to squeeze off any remaining moisture, sprinkle salt and black pepper on both sides of the scallops.
3. In a small bowl, mix the melted butter, minced garlic, chopped parsley, and lemon zest.
4. Spread a thin amount of olive oil into the air fryer basket, then add the scallops one at a time.
5. Brush the scallops with the herb butter mixture.
6. Air fry the scallops for 6-8 minutes, flipping halfway through, until they are golden brown and slightly firm to the touch.
7. Remove the scallops from the air fryer and serve hot with lemon wedges for a refreshing, keto-friendly seafood dish!

Zucchini and Crab-Stuffed Mushrooms

	Time: 25 minutes		Serving Size: 4 servings
	Prep Time: 10 minutes		Cook Time: 15 minutes

Nutrition Information Per Serving (1 serving unit (3 mushrooms)):

Calories: 160, Carbohydrates: 4g, Saturated Fat: 4g, Protein: 15g, Fat: 10g, Sodium: 480mg, Potassium: 450mg, Fiber: 1g, Sugar: 2g, Vitamin C: 3mg, Calcium: 40mg, Iron: 1mg.

Ingredients:
- 12 large mushrooms, stems removed
- 1/2 cup zucchini, finely diced
- 1/2 cup lump crab meat
- 1/4 cup cream cheese, softened
- 2 tbsp grated Parmesan cheese
- 1 tbsp fresh parsley, chopped
- 1 clove garlic, minced
- Salt and black pepper to taste
- Olive oil spray
- Lemon wedges for serving

Directions:
1. Preheat your air fryer to 375°F.
2. In a medium bowl, combine the diced zucchini, crab meat, cream cheese, Parmesan cheese, parsley, garlic, salt, and black pepper. Mix until fully incorporated.
3. Gently press the crab and zucchini mixture into each mushroom cap to ensure it is fully filled.
4. The stuffed mushrooms should be arranged in a single layer in the air fryer basket after lightly misting it with olive oil.
5. Bake for 12 to 15 minutes, or until the filling is bubbling and brown and the mushrooms are soft.
6. Take it out of the air fryer and serve warm with lemon wedges for a cool, keto-friendly snack. Enjoy!

Air-Fried Calamari Rings

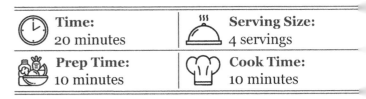

	Time: 20 minutes		Serving Size: 4 servings
	Prep Time: 10 minutes		Cook Time: 10 minutes

Nutrition Information Per Serving (1 serving unit):

Calories: 180, Carbohydrates: 4g, Saturated Fat: 2g, Protein: 23g, Fat: 8g, Sodium: 450mg, Potassium: 320mg, Fiber: 1g, Sugar: 0g, Vitamin C: 2mg, Calcium: 25mg, Iron: 1mg.

Ingredients:
- 1 lb calamari rings, cleaned
- 1/2 cup almond flour
- 1/4 cup grated Parmesan cheese
- 1 tsp smoked paprika
- 1/2 tsp garlic powder
- 1/2 tsp onion powder
- Salt and black pepper to taste
- 1 large egg, beaten
- Olive oil spray
- Lemon wedges for serving
- Keto-friendly marinara sauce (optional)

Directions:
1. Preheat your air fryer to 375°F.
2. In a shallow bowl, combine the almond flour, Parmesan cheese, smoked paprika, garlic powder, onion powder, salt, and black pepper.
3. To ensure a uniform coating, dip each calamari ring into the beaten egg and then coat it in the almond flour mixture.
4. Spread a thin amount of olive oil inside the air fryer basket and line it with calamari rings.
5. Air fry for 8-10 minutes, flipping halfway through, until the calamari is golden brown and crispy.
6. Serve hot with lemon wedges and keto-friendly marinara sauce for dipping. Enjoy these crispy, keto-friendly calamari rings as a light seafood snack or appetizer!

Keto Smoked Salmon Avocado Boats

🕐	Time: 10 minutes	🍽	Serving Size: 2 plates
🥗	Prep Time: 5 minutes	👨‍🍳	Cook Time: 5 minutes

Nutrition Information Per Serving (1 plate):

Calories: 320, Carbohydrates: 6g, Saturated Fat: 4g, Protein: 14g, Fat: 28g, Sodium: 420mg, Potassium: 680mg, Fiber: 5g, Sugar: 1g, Vitamin C: 12mg, Calcium: 30mg, Iron: 1mg.

Ingredients:

- 1 large ripe avocado, halved and pitted
- 3 oz smoked salmon, cut into small strips
- 2 tbsp cream cheese, softened
- 1 tbsp fresh dill, chopped
- 1 tsp lemon zest
- 1 tbsp capers, drained
- Salt and black pepper to taste
- Lemon wedges for serving

Directions:

1. Preheat your air fryer to 350°F.
2. Scoop out a little of the avocado flesh to create a larger well in each half, and set aside the extra avocado for another use.
3. In a small bowl, mix the cream cheese, lemon zest, and chopped dill until well combined.
4. Gently fold the smoked salmon strips into the cream cheese mixture.
5. Fill each avocado half with the smoked salmon mixture, then top with capers.
6. Place the avocado boats into the air fryer basket and air fry for 5 minutes, just enough to warm them through.
7. Season with salt and black pepper to taste, and serve immediately with lemon wedges for a fresh, keto-friendly dish that's packed with healthy fats and protein. Enjoy!

Air-Fried Clams with Garlic Butter

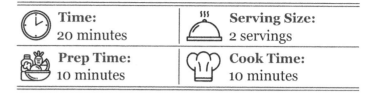

🕐	Time: 20 minutes	🍽	Serving Size: 2 servings
🥗	Prep Time: 10 minutes	👨‍🍳	Cook Time: 10 minutes

Nutrition Information Per Serving (1 serving unit):

Calories: 240, Carbohydrates: 4g, Saturated Fat: 6g, Protein: 18g, Fat: 15g, Sodium: 680mg, Potassium: 320mg, Fiber: 0g, Sugar: 0g, Vitamin C: 2mg, Calcium: 50mg, Iron: 5mg.

Ingredients:

- 1 lb fresh clams, scrubbed and cleaned
- 3 tbsp unsalted butter, melted
- 2 cloves garlic, minced
- 1 tbsp fresh parsley, chopped
- 1 tsp lemon zest
- Salt and black pepper to taste
- Olive oil spray
- Lemon wedges for serving

Directions:

1. Preheat your air fryer to 375°F.
2. Combine the melted butter, chopped parsley, lemon zest, and minced garlic in a small bowl. To taste, add salt and black pepper for seasoning.
3. After giving the cleaned clams a quick spray of olive oil in the air fryer basket, place them in a single layer.
4. Partially drizzle the clams with half of the garlic butter blend.
5. Air fry for 8-10 minutes, or until the clams open fully and are cooked through. Discard any clams that do not open.
6. Remove the clams from the air fryer and drizzle with the remaining garlic butter.
7. Serve hot with lemon wedges for a delicious, keto-friendly seafood dish packed with protein and healthy fats. Enjoy!

Chapter 7: Side dishes

Crispy Cauliflower Tots

⏰ Time: 25 minutes	🍽 Serving Size: 4 plates
🥗 Prep Time: 10 minutes	👨‍🍳 Cook Time: 15 minutes

Nutrition Information Per Serving (1 plate):
Calories: 120, Carbohydrates: 5g, Saturated Fat: 3g, Protein: 6g, Fat: 8g, Sodium: 310mg, Potassium: 280mg, Fiber: 2g, Sugar: 2g, Vitamin C: 30mg, Calcium: 80mg, Iron: 1mg.

Ingredients:
- 2 cups cauliflower florets, steamed and finely chopped
- 1/2 cup shredded cheddar cheese
- 1/4 cup grated Parmesan cheese
- 1 large egg, beaten
- 2 tbsp almond flour
- 1/2 tsp garlic powder
- 1/2 tsp onion powder
- Salt and black pepper to taste
- Olive oil spray

Directions:
1. Preheat your air fryer to 375°F.
2. In a large bowl, combine the steamed and finely chopped cauliflower, cheddar cheese, Parmesan cheese, beaten egg, almond flour, garlic powder, onion powder, salt, and black pepper. Mix until well combined.
3. Shape the mixture into small, bite-sized tots using your hands.
4. Spread the cauliflower tots in a single layer in the air fryer basket after giving it a quick spray of olive oil.
5. The tots should air fried for 12 to 15 minutes, turning them halfway through, or until they are crispy and golden brown.
6. Remove the tots from the air fryer and serve hot as a delicious and low-carb side dish or snack. Enjoy your keto-friendly cauliflower tots!

Garlic Parmesan Asparagus Spears

Time: 15 minutes	Serving Size: 4 servings
Prep Time: 5 minutes	Cook Time: 10 minutes

Nutrition Information Per Serving (1 serving unit):

Calories: 110, Carbohydrates: 5g, Saturated Fat: 3g, Protein: 5g, Fat: 8g, Sodium: 220mg, Potassium: 300mg, Fiber: 2g, Sugar: 1g, Vitamin C: 6mg, Calcium: 100mg, Iron: 2mg.

Ingredients:

- 1 bunch of fresh asparagus spears, trimmed
- 2 tbsp olive oil
- 1/4 cup grated Parmesan cheese
- 2 cloves garlic, minced
- 1/2 tsp garlic powder
- Salt and black pepper to taste
- Lemon wedges for serving

Directions:

1. Preheat your air fryer to 375°F.
2. The asparagus spears should be evenly coated after being mixed with olive oil, salt, black pepper, chopped garlic, and garlic powder in a big bowl.
3. Fill the air fryer basket with the asparagus stalks arranged in a single layer.
4. Air fry for 8-10 minutes, shaking the basket halfway through, until the asparagus is tender and lightly crispy.
5. In the final two minutes of cooking, toss the asparagus with the grated Parmesan cheese.
6. After taking the asparagus out of the air fryer, pour some fresh lemon juice over it before serving it hot for a zesty garnish. Enjoy your keto-friendly garlic Parmesan asparagus spears!

Cheesy Broccoli Bites

Time: 20 minutes	Serving Size: 4 servings
Prep Time: 10 minutes	Cook Time: 10 minutes

Nutrition Information Per Serving (1 serving unit):

Calories: 150, Carbohydrates: 5g, Saturated Fat: 4g, Protein: 8g, Fat: 10g, Sodium: 320mg, Potassium: 300mg, Fiber: 2g, Sugar: 1g, Vitamin C: 30mg, Calcium: 120mg, Iron: 1mg.

Ingredients:

- 2 cups broccoli florets, steamed and finely chopped
- 1/2 cup shredded cheddar cheese
- 1/4 cup grated Parmesan cheese
- 1 large egg, beaten
- 1/4 cup almond flour
- 1/2 tsp garlic powder
- 1/2 tsp onion powder
- Salt and black pepper to taste
- Olive oil spray

Directions:

1. Preheat your air fryer to 375°F.
2. In a large bowl, combine the steamed and finely chopped broccoli, cheddar cheese, Parmesan cheese, beaten egg, almond flour, garlic powder, onion powder, salt, and black pepper. Mix until well combined.
3. Little, bite-sized balls or patties should be formed from the mixture.
4. Spread a thin amount of olive oil within the air fryer basket, then line up the broccoli bites in a single layer.
5. Air fry for 8-10 minutes, flipping halfway through, until the bites are golden brown and crispy.
6. Serve hot as a side dish or snack, enjoying the cheesy goodness with every bite. Perfect for a low-carb, keto-friendly meal!

Air-Fried Brussels Sprouts with Bacon

 Time:
25 minutes

 Serving Size:
4 plates

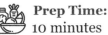 **Prep Time:**
10 minutes

 Cook Time:
15 minutes

Nutrition Information Per Serving (1 plate):

Calories: 180, Carbohydrates: 6g, Saturated Fat: 3g, Protein: 6g, Fat: 15g, Sodium: 380mg, Potassium: 350mg, Fiber: 3g, Sugar: 2g, Vitamin C: 55mg, Calcium: 40mg, Iron: 1mg.

Ingredients:

- 1 lb Brussels sprouts, halved
- 4 slices bacon, chopped
- 2 tbsp olive oil
- 1 tsp garlic powder
- ½ tsp smoked paprika
- ½ tsp sea salt
- ¼ tsp black pepper
- 1 tbsp balsamic vinegar (optional)

Directions:

1. Preheat your air fryer to 375°F.
2. The Brussels sprouts should be cut in half and combined with olive oil, smoked paprika, garlic powder, salt, and black pepper in a big bowl.
3. Toss to evenly spread the diced bacon throughout the Brussels sprouts combination.
4. Place the Brussels sprouts and bacon mixture in the air fryer basket in a single layer.
5. Crispy Brussels sprouts and cooked bacon can be achieved by air-frying them for 12 to 15 minutes, shaking the basket halfway through.
6. If preferred, drizzle with balsamic vinegar right before serving. Enjoy!

Cauliflower Mac and Cheese

 Time:
25 minutes

 Serving Size:
4 bowls

 Prep Time:
10 minutes

 Cook Time:
15 minutes

Nutrition Information Per Serving (1 bowl):

Calories: 220, Carbohydrates: 6g, Saturated Fat: 8g, Protein: 12g, Fat: 18g, Sodium: 450mg, Potassium: 320mg, Fiber: 3g, Sugar: 2g, Vitamin C: 50mg, Calcium: 200mg, Iron: 1mg.

Ingredients:

- 1 medium head of cauliflower, cut into small florets
- 1/2 cup heavy cream
- 1 cup shredded cheddar cheese
- 1/4 cup grated Parmesan cheese
- 2 tbsp cream cheese
- 1/2 tsp garlic powder
- 1/2 tsp onion powder
- Salt and black pepper to taste
- Olive oil spray
- Fresh parsley for garnish (optional)

Directions:

1. Preheat your air fryer to 375°F.
2. After around five minutes of steaming, the cauliflower florets should be soft but not mushy. After draining, set away.
3. Combine heavy cream, shredded cheddar, Parmesan, and cream cheese in a small saucepan over medium heat. Once the cheese has melted completely and the mixture is smooth, stir. Add salt, black pepper, onion powder, and garlic powder to taste. Toss the steamed cauliflower with the cheese sauce until well coated.
4. Transfer the cheesy cauliflower to an air fryer-safe dish and place it in the air fryer basket.
5. Air fry for 8-10 minutes until the top is golden and slightly crispy.
6. If preferred, garnish with fresh parsley and serve hot. Enjoy your keto-friendly cauliflower mac and cheese, a low-carb twist on a classic comfort food!

Keto «Breaded» Green Beans

⏰ Time: 20 minutes	🍽 Serving Size: 4 servings
🥗 Prep Time: 5 minutes	👨‍🍳 Cook Time: 15 minutes

Nutrition Information Per Serving (1 serving unit):
Calories: 120, Carbohydrates: 5g, Saturated Fat: 2g, Protein: 6g, Fat: 8g, Sodium: 300mg, Potassium: 180mg, Fiber: 2g, Sugar: 2g, Vitamin C: 15mg, Calcium: 90mg, Iron: 1mg.

Ingredients:

- 1 lb fresh green beans, trimmed
- 1/2 cup almond flour
- 1/4 cup grated Parmesan cheese
- 1 tsp garlic powder
- 1/2 tsp smoked paprika
- 1/4 tsp cayenne pepper (optional for extra spice)
- 1 large egg
- Olive oil spray
- Salt and black pepper to taste

Directions:

1. Preheat your air fryer to 375°F.
2. Add a dash of salt and black pepper to the egg while whisking it in a small basin.
3. In a separate bowl, mix the almond flour, Parmesan cheese, garlic powder, smoked paprika, cayenne pepper (if using), and a bit of salt and black pepper.
4. Gently press each green bean after dipping it in the egg wash and coating it with the almond flour mixture to make sure it adheres.
5. Place the breaded green beans in the air fryer basket in a single layer. Lightly spray them with olive oil to encourage crisping.
6. Air fry for 12-15 minutes, shaking the basket halfway through, until the green beans are golden and crispy.
7. Serve immediately as a tasty, low-carb side dish or snack. Enjoy your crispy keto green beans, a perfect guilt-free alternative to traditional breaded veggies!

Zucchini Parmesan Crisps

⏰ Time: 20 minutes	🍽 Serving Size: 4 servings
🥗 Prep Time: 5 minutes	👨‍🍳 Cook Time: 15 minutes

Nutrition Information Per Serving (1 serving unit):
Calories: 120, Carbohydrates: 4g, Saturated Fat: 2g, Protein: 7g, Fat: 8g, Sodium: 280mg, Potassium: 250mg, Fiber: 2g, Sugar: 2g, Vitamin C: 14mg, Calcium: 90mg, Iron: 1mg.

Ingredients:

- 2 medium zucchinis, thinly sliced into rounds
- 1/2 cup grated Parmesan cheese
- 1/4 cup almond flour
- 1 tsp Italian seasoning
- 1/2 tsp garlic powder
- Salt and black pepper to taste
- Olive oil spray

Directions:

1. Preheat your air fryer to 375°F.
2. In a small bowl, combine the Parmesan cheese, almond flour, Italian seasoning, garlic powder, salt, and black pepper.
3. Using a paper towel, pat the zucchini slices dry to absorb any remaining moisture.
4. Coat every zucchini slice uniformly on both sides by dipping it into the Parmesan mixture. To make sure the coating adheres, lightly press.
5. Make sure the breaded zucchini slices do not overlap when you arrange them in the air fryer basket in a single layer. Use a little olive oil spray.
6. The zucchini crisps should be air-fried for 12 to 15 minutes, turning them halfway through, or until they are golden and crisp.
7. Serve immediately for a delicious and keto-friendly side dish or snack. Enjoy your crispy Zucchini Parmesan Crisps as a flavorful, low-carb treat!

Air-Fried Mushrooms with Thyme

⏰ Time: 15 minutes	🍽 Serving Size: 4 plates
🥗 Prep Time: 5 minutes	👨‍🍳 Cook Time: 10 minutes

Nutrition Information Per Serving (1 plate):
Calories: 90, Carbohydrates: 4g, Saturated Fat: 2g, Protein: 3g, Fat: 7g, Sodium: 150mg, Potassium: 280mg, Fiber: 2g, Sugar: 1g, Vitamin C: 1mg, Calcium: 15mg, Iron: 1mg.

Ingredients:
- 10 oz baby Bella mushrooms, cleaned and halved
- 2 tbsp olive oil
- 1 tsp fresh thyme leaves (or 1/2 tsp dried thyme)
- 1/2 tsp garlic powder
- Salt and black pepper to taste
- 1 tbsp grated Parmesan cheese (optional)

Directions:
1. Preheat your air fryer to 375°F.
2. In a medium bowl, toss the halved mushrooms with olive oil, fresh thyme leaves, garlic powder, salt, and black pepper until evenly coated.
3. Fill the air fryer basket with the mushrooms arranged in a single layer. Avoid overcrowding for even cooking.
4. Shake the basket midway through the 8 to 10 minute air fry time, or until the mushrooms are soft and golden brown.
5. If desired, sprinkle the grated Parmesan cheese over the mushrooms during the last 2 minutes of cooking for added flavor.
6. Serve your Air-Fried Mushrooms with Thyme immediately as a savory, keto-friendly side dish or appetizer. Enjoy!

Spicy Jalapeño Cauliflower Rice

⏰ Time: 20 minutes	🍽 Serving Size: 4 bowls
🥗 Prep Time: 10 minutes	👨‍🍳 Cook Time: 10 minutes

Nutrition Information Per Serving (1 bowl):
Calories: 120, Carbohydrates: 6g, Saturated Fat: 3g, Protein: 4g, Fat: 10g, Sodium: 300mg, Potassium: 240mg, Fiber: 3g, Sugar: 2g, Vitamin C: 40mg, Calcium: 20mg, Iron: 1mg.

Ingredients:
- 1 medium head of cauliflower, grated (or 4 cups cauliflower rice)
- 2 tbsp olive oil
- 1 small jalapeño, finely chopped (seeds removed for less heat)
- 1/2 tsp garlic powder
- 1/2 tsp smoked paprika
- 1/4 tsp cumin
- Salt and black pepper to taste
- 1/4 cup shredded cheddar cheese (optional)
- 2 tbsp chopped fresh cilantro for garnish

Directions:
1. Preheat your air fryer to 375°F.
2. In a large bowl, combine the grated cauliflower with olive oil, chopped jalapeño, garlic powder, smoked paprika, cumin, salt, and black pepper. Toss well to coat the cauliflower in a uniform layer of spices.
3. Evenly distribute the cauliflower mixture within the air fryer basket. Cook for 8-10 minutes, shaking the basket halfway through to ensure even cooking.
4. If using cheese, sprinkle the shredded cheddar over the cauliflower during the last 2 minutes of cooking, allowing it to melt.
5. Once the cauliflower rice is tender and slightly crispy, remove from the air fryer and garnish with chopped cilantro.
6. Serve your Spicy Jalapeño Cauliflower Rice as a flavorful, keto-friendly side dish. Enjoy!

Crispy Air-Fried Radishes

Time: 25 minutes	Serving Size: 4 plates
Prep Time: 10 minutes	Cook Time: 15 minutes

Nutrition Information Per Serving (1 plate):

Calories: 65, Carbohydrates: 5g, Saturated Fat: 2g, Protein: 1g, Fat: 6g, Sodium: 200mg, Potassium: 180mg, Fiber: 2g, Sugar: 2g, Vitamin C: 15mg, Calcium: 30mg, Iron: 0.5mg.

Ingredients:

- 2 cups radishes, trimmed and halved
- 2 tbsp olive oil
- 1/2 tsp garlic powder
- 1/2 tsp smoked paprika
- 1/4 tsp sea salt
- 1/4 tsp black pepper
- 2 tbsp grated Parmesan cheese
- Fresh parsley, chopped (optional for garnish)

Directions:

1. Preheat your air fryer to 375°F.
2. Sea salt, black pepper, smoked paprika, garlic powder, and olive oil should all be combined and mixed evenly with the halved radishes in a big mixing basin.
3. Arrange the seasoned radishes in the air fryer basket in a single layer. Fry the radishes for 12 to 15 minutes, shaking the basket halfway through, or until the outsides are crispy and golden brown.
4. Sprinkle the Parmesan cheese over the radishes during the last 2 minutes of cooking to allow it to melt and form a crispy coating.
5. After they are cooked, take the radishes out of the air fryer and place them on a platter for serving. If desired, garnish with fresh parsley.
6. Serve your Crispy Air-Fried Radishes as a keto-friendly side dish or snack, perfect for adding a crunchy and savory bite to any meal. Enjoy!

Roasted Garlic Cauliflower Mash

Time: 30 minutes	Serving Size: 4 bowls
Prep Time: 10 minutes	Cook Time: 20 minutes

Nutrition Information Per Serving (1 bowl):

Calories: 130, Carbohydrates: 6g, Saturated Fat: 4g, Protein: 3g, Fat: 10g, Sodium: 220mg, Potassium: 330mg, Fiber: 3g, Sugar: 2g, Vitamin C: 55mg, Calcium: 40mg, Iron: 1mg.

Ingredients:

- 1 large head of cauliflower, cut into florets
- 4 cloves garlic, peeled
- 2 tbsp olive oil
- 2 tbsp unsalted butter
- 1/4 cup heavy cream
- 1/4 cup grated Parmesan cheese
- 1/4 tsp sea salt
- 1/4 tsp black pepper
- Fresh chives, chopped (optional for garnish)

Directions:

1. Preheat your air fryer to 375°F.
2. In a mixing bowl, toss the cauliflower florets and garlic cloves with olive oil, ensuring they are evenly coated.
3. Spread the cauliflower and garlic in a single layer in the air fryer basket. Cook for 15-18 minutes, shaking halfway through, until the cauliflower is tender and lightly golden.
4. Once roasted, transfer the cauliflower and garlic to a food processor. Add the butter, heavy cream, Parmesan cheese, sea salt, and black pepper. Blend until smooth and creamy.
5. Adjust the seasoning to taste and pulse again if necessary to reach the desired consistency.
6. Spoon the Roasted Garlic Cauliflower Mash into a serving dish and garnish with fresh chives if desired.
7. Serve as a low-carb alternative to mashed potatoes, pairing perfectly with your favorite keto-friendly main dishes. Enjoy!

Avocado Stuffed with Creamy Crab

	Time: 15 minutes		Serving Size: 2 stuffed of avocado
	Prep Time: 10 minutes		Cook Time: 5 minutes

Nutrition Information Per Serving (1 stuffed halve of avocado):

Calories: 260, Carbohydrates: 6g, Saturated Fat: 3g, Protein: 15g, Fat: 22g, Sodium: 350mg, Potassium: 485mg, Fiber: 5g, Sugar: 1g, Vitamin C: 15mg, Calcium: 45mg, Iron: 1.5mg.

Ingredients:

- 1 large ripe avocado, halved and pitted
- 4 oz lump crab meat
- 2 tbsp mayonnaise
- 1 tsp Dijon mustard
- 1/2 tsp lemon juice
- 1 tbsp fresh chives, chopped
- 1/4 tsp paprika
- Salt and pepper to taste
- Lemon wedges (for serving)

Directions:

1. Preheat your air fryer to 375°F.
2. In a medium bowl, mix together the crab meat, mayonnaise, Dijon mustard, lemon juice, chives, paprika, salt, and pepper. Stir until well combined and creamy.
3. Scoop out a small portion of the avocado flesh from the center of each half to create more space for the filling. Set aside the scooped avocado.
4. Gently fold the reserved avocado into the crab mixture.
5. Spoon the creamy crab mixture evenly into the hollowed avocado halves.
6. Place the stuffed avocados in the air fryer basket and cook for 4-5 minutes until warmed through.
7. Serve immediately with a sprinkle of fresh chives and a lemon wedge on the side for added flavor. Enjoy this nutritious, keto-friendly side dish!

Keto Cheddar Zucchini Cakes

	Time: 25 minutes		Serving Size: 4 cakes
	Prep Time: 10 minutes		Cook Time: 15 minutes

Nutrition Information Per Serving (1 cake):

Calories: 150, Carbohydrates: 4g, Saturated Fat: 4g, Protein: 7g, Fat: 12g, Sodium: 320mg, Potassium: 220mg, Fiber: 1g, Sugar: 2g, Vitamin C: 15mg, Calcium: 140mg, Iron: 1.2mg.

Ingredients:

- 2 medium zucchinis, grated
- 1/2 cup shredded cheddar cheese
- 1 large egg
- 1/4 cup almond flour
- 1/2 tsp garlic powder
- 1/4 tsp onion powder
- 1/4 tsp smoked paprika
- Salt and pepper to taste
- 1 tbsp olive oil (for brushing)

Directions:

1. Preheat the air fryer to 375°F.
2. Grate the zucchini and use a fresh kitchen towel to wring out any extra moisture.
3. In a medium bowl, combine the grated zucchini, cheddar cheese, egg, almond flour, garlic powder, onion powder, smoked paprika, salt, and pepper. Mix until well combined.
4. Form the zucchini mixture into small patties, about 2 inches in diameter.
5. Lightly brush the patties with olive oil on both sides.
6. Place the zucchini cakes in a single layer in the air fryer basket. Air-fry for 10-12 minutes, flipping halfway through, until golden brown and crispy.
7. Warm it up for a snack or side dish and enjoy it with your favorite keto-friendly dip or a dollop of sour cream. Enjoy!

Cabbage and Bacon Crisps

Time: 25 minutes	Serving Size: 4 bowls
Prep Time: 10 minutes	Cook Time: 15 minutes

Nutrition Information Per Serving (1 bowl):
Calories: 180, Carbohydrates: 4g, Saturated Fat: 6g, Protein: 8g, Fat: 15g, Sodium: 450mg, Potassium: 300mg, Fiber: 2g, Sugar: 1g, Vitamin C: 35mg, Calcium: 40mg, Iron: 1mg.

Ingredients:

- 4 cups shredded green cabbage
- 4 slices of bacon, cooked and crumbled
- 1 tbsp olive oil
- 1 tsp garlic powder
- 1/2 tsp smoked paprika
- 1/2 tsp salt
- 1/4 tsp black pepper

Directions:

1. Preheat the air fryer to 375°F.
2. Combine olive oil, smoked paprika, garlic powder, salt, and pepper in a big bowl and toss to cover the shredded cabbage evenly.
3. Spread the cabbage mixture in an even layer in the air fryer basket. Air-fry for 10 minutes, shaking the basket halfway through to ensure even cooking.
4. After 10 minutes, add the crumbled bacon to the air fryer and cook for an additional 5 minutes, or until the cabbage is crispy and golden brown.
5. Serve hot as a crunchy side dish or snack.

Air-Fried Eggplant Rounds

Time: 20 minutes	Serving Size: 4 servings
Prep Time: 5 minutes	Cook Time: 15 minutes

Nutrition Information Per Serving (1 serving unit):
Calories: 120, Carbohydrates: 7g, Saturated Fat: 2g, Protein: 3g, Fat: 9g, Sodium: 210mg, Potassium: 320mg, Fiber: 3g, Sugar: 3g, Vitamin C: 2.4mg, Calcium: 20mg, Iron: 0.5mg.

Ingredients:

- 1 medium eggplant, sliced into 1/2-inch rounds
- 2 tbsp olive oil
- 1/4 cup grated Parmesan cheese
- 1 tsp garlic powder
- 1 tsp paprika
- 1/2 tsp salt
- 1/2 tsp black pepper
- 1 tbsp fresh parsley, chopped (optional)

Directions:

1. Preheat your air fryer to 375°F.
2. In a bowl, mix the olive oil, garlic powder, paprika, salt, and black pepper.
3. Brush both sides of each eggplant round with the olive oil mixture.
4. Sprinkle Parmesan cheese evenly on top of each slice.
5. Place the eggplant rounds in a single layer in the air fryer basket.
6. Air-fry for 12-15 minutes until golden brown and crispy, flipping halfway through.
7. Remove from the air fryer, garnish with fresh parsley if desired, and serve warm.

Chapter 8: Plant-based

Air-Fried Eggplant Parmesan

Time: 30 minutes	Serving Size: 4 plates
Prep Time: 10 minutes	Cook Time: 20 minutes

Nutrition Information Per Serving (1 plate):
Calories: 220, Carbohydrates: 10g, Saturated Fat: 4g, Protein: 10g, Fat: 15g, Sodium: 500mg, Potassium: 450mg, Fiber: 5g, Sugar: 4g, Vitamin C: 8mg, Calcium: 150mg, Iron: 2mg.

Ingredients:
- 1 medium eggplant, sliced into 1/4-inch rounds
- 1 cup almond flour
- 1/2 cup grated Parmesan cheese
- 1 tsp garlic powder
- 1 tsp dried oregano
- 1/2 tsp salt
- 1/4 tsp black pepper
- 2 large eggs, beaten
- 1 cup sugar-free marinara sauce
- 1/2 cup shredded mozzarella cheese
- Fresh basil leaves for garnish (optional)

Directions:
1. Preheat your air fryer to 375°F.
2. In a bowl, combine the almond flour, grated Parmesan cheese, garlic powder, oregano, salt, and black pepper.
3. Dip each eggplant slice into the beaten eggs, then coat them in the almond flour mixture, pressing gently to adhere.
4. Arrange the coated eggplant slices in the air fryer basket in a single layer. Air-fry for 12-15 minutes, flipping halfway through, until the eggplant is golden and crispy.
5. Once the eggplant is done, top each slice with a spoonful of marinara sauce and a sprinkle of shredded mozzarella cheese. Air-fry for an additional 3-5 minutes until the cheese is melted and bubbly.
6. Serve garnished with fresh basil leaves if desired.

Zucchini Noodles with Pesto

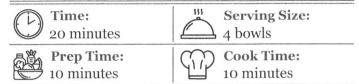

🕐	**Time:** 20 minutes	🍽	**Serving Size:** 4 bowls
🥗	**Prep Time:** 10 minutes	👨‍🍳	**Cook Time:** 10 minutes

Nutrition Information Per Serving (1 bowl):

Calories: 180, Carbohydrates: 6g, Saturated Fat: 2g, Protein: 4g, Fat: 16g, Sodium: 180mg, Potassium: 500mg, Fiber: 2g, Sugar: 4g, Vitamin C: 20mg, Calcium: 50mg, Iron: 1mg.

Ingredients:

- 4 medium zucchini, spiralized
- 1/2 cup fresh basil leaves
- 1/4 cup pine nuts
- 1/4 cup grated Parmesan cheese
- 1 garlic clove, minced
- 1/2 cup olive oil
- 1 tbsp lemon juice
- Salt and pepper to taste
- 1/4 tsp red pepper flakes (optional)

Directions:

1. Preheat your air fryer to 350°F.
2. In a blender or food processor, combine basil leaves, pine nuts, grated Parmesan cheese, garlic, olive oil, lemon juice, salt, and pepper. Blend until smooth to make the pesto sauce.
3. Toss the spiralized zucchini noodles with the pesto until well coated.
4. Place the zucchini noodles in the air fryer basket and cook for 8-10 minutes, tossing halfway through, until the noodles are slightly tender but still firm.
5. Serve immediately, garnished with red pepper flakes if desired.

Crispy Cauliflower Steaks

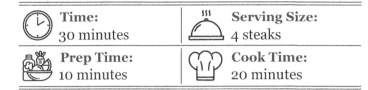

🕐	**Time:** 30 minutes	🍽	**Serving Size:** 4 steaks
🥗	**Prep Time:** 10 minutes	👨‍🍳	**Cook Time:** 20 minutes

Nutrition Information Per Serving (1 steak):

Calories: 180, Carbohydrates: 9g, Saturated Fat: 2g, Protein: 5g, Fat: 14g, Sodium: 320mg, Potassium: 450mg, Fiber: 4g, Sugar: 3g, Vitamin C: 40mg, Calcium: 60mg, Iron: 1.5mg.

Ingredients:

- 1 large cauliflower head, sliced into 1-inch steaks
- 2 tbsps olive oil
- 1 tsp smoked paprika
- 1 tsp garlic powder
- 1/2 tsp onion powder
- 1/4 tsp black pepper
- 1/4 tsp sea salt
- 1/4 cup almond flour
- 2 tbsps nutritional yeast (optional, for cheesy flavor)

Directions:

1. Preheat your air fryer to 375°F.
2. In a small bowl, mix olive oil, smoked paprika, garlic powder, onion powder, black pepper, and sea salt.
3. Brush both sides of the cauliflower steaks with the seasoned olive oil mixture.
4. In another bowl, combine almond flour and nutritional yeast. Gently press the cauliflower steaks into the mixture, coating both sides evenly.
5. Place the cauliflower steaks in the air fryer basket in a single layer. Cook for 15-20 minutes, flipping halfway through, until golden and crispy on the edges.
6. Serve immediately as a delicious and satisfying plant-based main or side dish.

Air-Fried Tofu with Chili Lime

⏰ Time: 25 minutes	🍽 Serving Size: 4 plates
🥗 Prep Time: 10 minutes	👨‍🍳 Cook Time: 15 minutes

Nutrition Information Per Serving (1 plate):

Calories: 210, Carbohydrates: 4g, Saturated Fat: 2g, Protein: 16g, Fat: 15g, Sodium: 400mg, Potassium: 200mg, Fiber: 1g, Sugar: 1g, Vitamin C: 8mg, Calcium: 220mg, Iron: 3mg.

Ingredients:

- 1 block firm tofu, pressed and cut into 1-inch cubes
- 2 tbsps olive oil
- 1 tbsp lime juice
- 1 tsp chili powder
- 1/2 tsp garlic powder
- 1/2 tsp cumin
- 1/4 tsp paprika
- 1/4 tsp sea salt
- 1/4 tsp black pepper
- Zest of 1 lime
- Fresh cilantro for garnish

Directions:

1. Preheat your air fryer to 375°F.
2. In a bowl, whisk together olive oil, lime juice, chili powder, garlic powder, cumin, paprika, sea salt, and black pepper.
3. Toss the tofu cubes in the marinade, ensuring they are evenly coated. Let them sit for 5 minutes to absorb the flavors.
4. Place the tofu cubes in a single layer in the air fryer basket and cook for 12-15 minutes, shaking the basket halfway through, until the tofu is crispy and golden.
5. Once cooked, sprinkle with lime zest and garnish with fresh cilantro. Serve as a protein-packed plant-based dish with a zesty kick.

Stuffed Bell Peppers with Cauliflower Rice

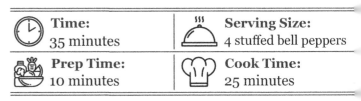

⏰ Time: 35 minutes	🍽 Serving Size: 4 stuffed bell peppers
🥗 Prep Time: 10 minutes	👨‍🍳 Cook Time: 25 minutes

Nutrition Information Per Serving (1 stuffed bell pepper):

Calories: 180, Carbohydrates: 9g, Saturated Fat: 3g, Protein: 5g, Fat: 12g, Sodium: 350mg, Potassium: 380mg, Fiber: 3g, Sugar: 4g, Vitamin C: 90mg, Calcium: 40mg, Iron: 1.2mg.

Ingredients:

- 4 large bell peppers, tops removed and seeds cleaned
- 2 cups cauliflower rice
- 1/2 cup diced tomatoes
- 1/2 cup chopped spinach
- 1/4 cup diced onions
- 2 tbsps olive oil
- 1 tsp cumin
- 1/2 tsp garlic powder
- 1/2 tsp smoked paprika
- 1/4 tsp sea salt
- 1/4 tsp black pepper
- Fresh parsley for garnish

Directions:

1. Preheat your air fryer to 375°F.
2. In a pan, heat olive oil over medium heat. Add diced onions and sauté for 2-3 minutes until soft.
3. Stir in cauliflower rice, diced tomatoes, spinach, cumin, garlic powder, smoked paprika, sea salt, and black pepper. Cook for 5 minutes until the mixture is well combined.
4. Stuff the bell peppers with the cauliflower rice mixture, packing it firmly.
5. Place the stuffed peppers in the air fryer basket and cook for 20-25 minutes until the peppers are tender and slightly charred on the edges.
6. Garnish with fresh parsley and serve warm for a delicious and nutrient-packed plant-based dish.

Air-Fried Spaghetti Squash Boats

🕐	Time: 40 minutes	🍽	Serving Size: 2 halves of squash
🥗	Prep Time: 10 minutes	👨‍🍳	Cook Time: 30 minutes

Nutrition Information Per Serving (1 half of a squash):
Calories: 160, Carbohydrates: 12g, Saturated Fat: 3g, Protein: 4g, Fat: 11g, Sodium: 320mg, Potassium: 410mg, Fiber: 3g, Sugar: 5g, Vitamin C: 15mg, Calcium: 50mg, Iron: 1mg.

Ingredients:
- 1 medium spaghetti squash, halved and seeds removed
- 2 tbsps olive oil
- 1/2 cup cherry tomatoes, halved
- 1/4 cup fresh basil, chopped
- 1/4 cup grated Parmesan cheese
- 1 tsp garlic powder
- 1/2 tsp sea salt
- 1/4 tsp black pepper
- 1/4 tsp red pepper flakes (optional)

Directions:
1. Preheat your air fryer to 375°F.
2. Brush the inside of the spaghetti squash halves with olive oil and season with sea salt and black pepper.
3. Place the squash halves cut side up in the air fryer basket and cook for 25-30 minutes until the flesh is tender and easily scraped into strands with a fork.
4. While the squash cooks, in a bowl, mix cherry tomatoes, basil, garlic powder, and red pepper flakes (if using).
5. Once the squash is done, scrape the flesh into strands, keeping it inside the shell to form «boats.»
6. Top each squash half with the tomato mixture and sprinkle with grated Parmesan cheese. Return to the air fryer for an additional 5 minutes until the cheese melts and is golden.
7. Garnish with extra basil and serve warm for a satisfying, low-carb plant-based meal.

Keto Avocado Salad Cups

🕐	Time: 20 minutes	🍽	Serving Size: 4 avocado halves
🥗	Prep Time: 15 minutes	👨‍🍳	Cook Time: 5 minutes

Nutrition Information Per Serving (1 stuffed avocado half):
Calories: 210, Carbohydrates: 8g, Saturated Fat: 3g, Protein: 3g, Fat: 19g, Sodium: 240mg, Potassium: 420mg, Fiber: 6g, Sugar: 1g, Vitamin C: 15mg, Calcium: 25mg, Iron: 0.5mg.

Ingredients:
- 2 ripe avocados, halved and pitted
- 1 small cucumber, diced
- 1/4 cup red onion, finely chopped
- 1/4 cup cherry tomatoes, halved
- 1 tbsp olive oil
- 1 tbsp lime juice
- 1 tsp garlic powder
- 1/4 tsp sea salt
- 1/4 tsp black pepper
- 1 tbsp fresh cilantro, chopped (optional)

Directions:
1. Preheat the air fryer to 350°F.
2. Scoop out a bit of the avocado flesh from the center of each avocado half to create a cup shape. Set the scooped-out avocado aside for later use.
3. In a bowl, combine the diced cucumber, red onion, cherry tomatoes, and the scooped-out avocado.
4. Drizzle the olive oil and lime juice over the mixture, and sprinkle with garlic powder, sea salt, and black pepper. Stir gently to combine.
5. Spoon the salad mixture into the avocado cups.
6. Place the filled avocado halves into the air fryer basket and cook for 5 minutes, just until the filling is slightly warm and the avocado is lightly softened.
7. Remove from the air fryer, garnish with fresh cilantro if desired, and serve immediately.

Grilled Portobello Mushroom Caps

 Time: 25 minutes

 Serving Size: 4 mushrooms caps

 Prep Time: 10 minutes

Cook Time: 15 minutes

Nutrition Information Per Serving (1 mushroom cap):

Calories: 110, Carbohydrates: 5g, Saturated Fat: 2g, Protein: 3g, Fat: 9g, Sodium: 180mg, Potassium: 450mg, Fiber: 2g, Sugar: 1g, Vitamin C: 2mg, Calcium: 20mg, Iron: 0.5mg.

Ingredients:

- 4 large Portobello mushroom caps
- 2 tbsps olive oil
- 1 tbsp balsamic vinegar
- 2 cloves garlic, minced
- 1 tsp dried oregano
- 1 tsp smoked paprika
- 1/2 tsp sea salt
- 1/4 tsp black pepper
- Fresh parsley, chopped (for garnish)

Directions:

1. Preheat the air fryer to 375°F.
2. Clean the Portobello mushroom caps by gently wiping them with a damp cloth. Remove the stems and scrape out the gills using a spoon if desired.
3. In a small bowl, mix olive oil, balsamic vinegar, minced garlic, oregano, smoked paprika, sea salt, and black pepper to create a marinade.
4. Brush the marinade generously over both sides of each mushroom cap.
5. Place the mushroom caps in the air fryer basket, gill side down, and cook for 8 minutes.
6. Flip the mushroom caps and continue cooking for an additional 7 minutes until tender and slightly crispy on the edges.
7. Remove from the air fryer, garnish with fresh parsley, and serve immediately.

Zucchini Lasagna Rolls

 Time: 35 minutes

 Serving Size: 4 servings

 Prep Time: 15 minutes

 Cook Time: 20 minutes

Nutrition Information Per Serving (1 serving unit):

Calories: 180, Carbohydrates: 6g, Saturated Fat: 3g, Protein: 7g, Fat: 14g, Sodium: 320mg, Potassium: 470mg, Fiber: 2g, Sugar: 4g, Vitamin C: 12mg, Calcium: 80mg, Iron: 1mg.

Ingredients:

- 2 large zucchinis, thinly sliced lengthwise
- 1 cup marinara sauce (keto-friendly)
- 1 cup ricotta cheese
- 1/4 cup grated Parmesan cheese
- 1 tbsp olive oil
- 1 tsp dried basil
- 1 tsp garlic powder
- 1/4 tsp red pepper flakes
- 1/4 tsp salt
- Fresh basil, chopped (for garnish)

Directions:

1. Preheat the air fryer to 350°F.
2. Using a mandoline or sharp knife, slice the zucchini lengthwise into thin strips.
3. In a bowl, mix ricotta cheese, Parmesan cheese, dried basil, garlic powder, red pepper flakes, and salt. Stir until smooth.
4. Lay the zucchini strips flat and spoon a tbsp of the ricotta mixture onto one end of each strip. Roll each zucchini slice gently into a spiral and secure with a toothpick if necessary.
5. Spread a thin layer of marinara sauce on the bottom of the air fryer basket. Place the zucchini rolls seam-side down on top of the sauce.
6. Drizzle olive oil over the zucchini rolls and spoon the remaining marinara sauce over the top.
7. Air fry for 15-20 minutes until the zucchini is tender and the cheese is golden.
8. Remove from the air fryer and garnish with fresh chopped basil before serving.

Air-Fried Artichoke Hearts

⏱ **Time:** 25 minutes	🍽 **Serving Size:** 4 plates
🥗 **Prep Time:** 10 minutes	👨‍🍳 **Cook Time:** 15 minutes

Nutrition Information Per Serving (1 plate):
Calories: 120, Carbohydrates: 7g, Saturated Fat: 2g, Protein: 4g, Fat: 9g, Sodium: 240mg, Potassium: 230mg, Fiber: 4g, Sugar: 1g, Vitamin C: 10mg, Calcium: 40mg, Iron: 1.5mg.

Ingredients:

- 1 can (14 oz) artichoke hearts, drained and halved
- 1/2 cup almond flour
- 1/4 cup grated Parmesan cheese
- 1 tbsp olive oil
- 1 tsp garlic powder
- 1/2 tsp smoked paprika
- 1/4 tsp black pepper
- 1/4 tsp salt
- Fresh parsley, chopped (for garnish)
- Lemon wedges (for serving)

Directions:

1. Preheat the air fryer to 375°F.
2. Drain the artichoke hearts and pat them dry with paper towels to remove excess moisture.
3. In a bowl, mix almond flour, Parmesan cheese, garlic powder, smoked paprika, black pepper, and salt.
4. Drizzle olive oil over the artichoke hearts, tossing to coat evenly.
5. Roll each artichoke heart in the almond flour mixture, pressing gently to ensure an even coating.
6. Place the coated artichoke hearts in a single layer in the air fryer basket. Air fry for 12-15 minutes, turning halfway through, until golden and crispy.
7. Remove from the air fryer and sprinkle with fresh parsley. Serve with lemon wedges for a zesty finish.

Roasted Garlic Cauliflower Bites

⏱ **Time:** 25 minutes	🍽 **Serving Size:** 4 plates
🥗 **Prep Time:** 10 minutes	👨‍🍳 **Cook Time:** 15 minutes

Nutrition Information Per Serving (1 plate):
Calories: 110, Carbohydrates: 7g, Saturated Fat: 1.5g, Protein: 4g, Fat: 7g, Sodium: 230mg, Potassium: 280mg, Fiber: 3g, Sugar: 2g, Vitamin C: 45mg, Calcium: 35mg, Iron: 1mg.

Ingredients:

- 1 medium head of cauliflower, cut into bite-sized florets
- 3 tbsps olive oil
- 4 cloves garlic, minced
- 1/4 cup nutritional yeast (or grated Parmesan for non-vegan option)
- 1 tsp smoked paprika
- 1/2 tsp salt
- 1/4 tsp black pepper
- Fresh parsley, chopped (for garnish)
- Lemon wedges (for serving)

Directions:

1. Preheat the air fryer to 375°F.
2. In a large bowl, toss the cauliflower florets with olive oil, minced garlic, smoked paprika, salt, and black pepper.
3. Add the nutritional yeast or Parmesan to the mixture and stir until the cauliflower is well coated.
4. Place the cauliflower florets in a single layer in the air fryer basket. Air fry for 12-15 minutes, shaking the basket halfway through, until the cauliflower is golden and crispy.
5. Remove from the air fryer, sprinkle with fresh parsley, and serve with lemon wedges for a fresh, zesty flavor boost.

Air-Fried Brussels Sprout Chips

⏰ Time: 20 minutes	🍽 Serving Size: 4 servings
🥗 Prep Time: 5 minutes	👨‍🍳 Cook Time: 15 minutes

Nutrition Information Per Serving (1 serving unit):

Calories: 85, Carbohydrates: 6g, Saturated Fat: 1g, Protein: 3g, Fat: 6g, Sodium: 180mg, Potassium: 340mg, Fiber: 2g, Sugar: 1g, Vitamin C: 48mg, Calcium: 30mg, Iron: 1mg.

Ingredients:

- 1 pound Brussels sprouts
- 2 tbsps olive oil
- 1/2 tsp garlic powder
- 1/4 tsp smoked paprika
- 1/2 tsp sea salt
- 1/4 tsp black pepper
- Grated lemon zest (for garnish)
- Optional: red pepper flakes for extra spice

Directions:

1. Preheat the air fryer to 375°F.
2. Trim the ends off the Brussels sprouts and peel away the outer leaves. Place the loose leaves into a large bowl.
3. Drizzle olive oil over the Brussels sprout leaves and toss with garlic powder, smoked paprika, sea salt, and black pepper until well coated.
4. Spread the Brussels sprout leaves evenly in the air fryer basket. Air fry for 8-10 minutes, shaking the basket halfway through to ensure even crisping.
5. Once the leaves are golden and crispy, remove from the air fryer and sprinkle with grated lemon zest.
6. Optional: Add a pinch of red pepper flakes for extra heat. Serve immediately for a crunchy, low-carb snack!

Spiced Cabbage Steaks

⏰ Time: 25 minutes	🍽 Serving Size: 5 steaks
🥗 Prep Time: 5 minutes	👨‍🍳 Cook Time: 20 minutes

Nutrition Information Per Serving (1 steak):

Calories: 75, Carbohydrates: 7g, Saturated Fat: 1g, Protein: 2g, Fat: 6g, Sodium: 200mg, Potassium: 220mg, Fiber: 3g, Sugar: 3g, Vitamin C: 35mg, Calcium: 40mg, Iron: 0.8mg.

Ingredients:

- 1 medium green cabbage, cut into 1-inch thick rounds
- 2 tbsps olive oil
- 1 tsp smoked paprika
- 1/2 tsp ground cumin
- 1/2 tsp garlic powder
- 1/4 tsp cayenne
- pepper (optional, for heat)
- 1/2 tsp sea salt
- 1/4 tsp black pepper
- Fresh parsley, chopped (for garnish)
- Lemon wedges (for serving)

Directions:

1. Preheat the air fryer to 375°F.
2. In a small bowl, mix together the olive oil, smoked paprika, cumin, garlic powder, cayenne pepper (if using), sea salt, and black pepper.
3. Brush both sides of the cabbage steaks with the seasoned oil mixture, ensuring they are evenly coated.
4. Place the cabbage steaks in a single layer in the air fryer basket. Air fry for 15-20 minutes, flipping halfway through, until the edges are crispy and golden.
5. Once cooked, remove from the air fryer and garnish with fresh parsley.
6. Serve with lemon wedges for an extra burst of flavor.

Creamy Spinach and Cauliflower Gratin

 Time:
30 minutes

 Serving Size:
4 bowls

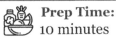 **Prep Time:**
10 minutes

 Cook Time:
20 minutes

Nutrition Information Per Serving (1 bowl):

Calories: 190, Carbohydrates: 6g, Saturated Fat: 6g, Protein: 7g, Fat: 15g, Sodium: 320mg, Potassium: 320mg, Fiber: 3g, Sugar: 2g, Vitamin C: 45mg, Calcium: 120mg, Iron: 1.2mg.

Ingredients:

- 1 small head of cauliflower, cut into small florets
- 2 cups fresh spinach, chopped
- 1/2 cup heavy cream
- 1/2 cup shredded mozzarella cheese
- 1/4 cup grated Parmesan cheese
- 2 tbsps cream cheese
- 1/2 tsp garlic powder
- 1/4 tsp ground nutmeg
- Salt and pepper to taste
- 1 tbsp olive oil
- Fresh thyme, for garnish

Directions:

1. Preheat the air fryer to 375°F.
2. Steam the cauliflower florets until tender, about 5-7 minutes. Drain and set aside.
3. In a small saucepan over medium heat, combine the heavy cream, cream cheese, garlic powder, nutmeg, salt, and pepper. Stir until smooth and creamy.
4. Add the chopped spinach to the cream mixture and cook until wilted, about 2-3 minutes.
5. In a mixing bowl, toss the steamed cauliflower with the creamy spinach mixture until well coated.
6. Transfer the mixture to a greased, air fryer-safe dish. Sprinkle with mozzarella and Parmesan cheese on top.
7. Air fry for 10-12 minutes or until the top is golden and bubbly.
8. Garnish with fresh thyme and serve warm.

Air-Fried Stuffed Avocados

 Time:
20 minutes

Serving Size:
2 stuffed avocados

 Prep Time:
10 minutes

 Cook Time:
10 minutes

Nutrition Information Per Serving (1 stuffed avocado):

Calories: 350, Carbohydrates: 8g, Saturated Fat: 6g, Protein: 7g, Fat: 33g, Sodium: 240mg, Potassium: 710mg, Fiber: 7g, Sugar: 1g, Vitamin C: 15mg, Calcium: 40mg, Iron: 1mg.

Ingredients:

- 2 ripe avocados, halved and pitted
- 1/2 cup cherry tomatoes, diced
- 1/4 cup red onion, finely chopped
- 2 tbsps fresh cilantro, chopped
- 2 tbsps lime juice
- 1/4 cup shredded mozzarella cheese
- 1 tbsp olive oil
- 1/4 tsp chili powder
- Salt and pepper to taste

Directions:

1. Preheat the air fryer to 350°F.
2. Scoop out a small portion of the avocado from each half, leaving enough flesh to hold the shape. Set the scooped-out avocado aside.
3. In a small bowl, combine the diced tomatoes, red onion, cilantro, lime juice, and the reserved avocado flesh. Season with chili powder, salt, and pepper. Mix well.
4. Fill each avocado half with the tomato mixture. Top with shredded mozzarella cheese.
5. Lightly brush the avocado skins with olive oil.
6. Air fry the stuffed avocados for 8-10 minutes or until the cheese is golden and bubbly.
7. Remove from the air fryer, garnish with extra cilantro, and serve warm.

Chapter 9: Desserts

Keto Air-Fried Donuts

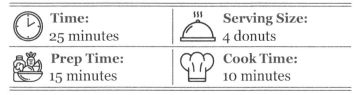 Time: 25 minutes	Serving Size: 4 donuts
Prep Time: 15 minutes	Cook Time: 10 minutes

Nutrition Information Per Serving (1 donut):

Calories: 210, Carbohydrates: 4g, Saturated Fat: 6g, Protein: 8g, Fat: 18g, Sodium: 150mg, Potassium: 130mg, Fiber: 3g, Sugar: 1g, Vitamin C: 0mg, Calcium: 60mg, Iron: 1mg.

Ingredients:
- 1 cup almond flour
- 2 tbsps coconut flour
- 1/4 cup erythritol (or preferred keto sweetener)
- 1 tsp baking powder
- 1/4 tsp ground cinnamon
- 1/4 cup unsweetened almond milk
- 2 large eggs
- 2 tbsps melted butter
- 1 tsp vanilla extract
- 1/4 tsp nutmeg (optional)
- Olive oil spray (for greasing the air fryer)

Directions:

1. Preheat the air fryer to 350°F.

2. In a medium bowl, whisk together the almond flour, coconut flour, erythritol, baking powder, cinnamon, and nutmeg.

3. In another bowl, whisk the eggs, melted butter, almond milk, and vanilla extract until smooth.

4. Gradually add the wet ingredients to the dry ingredients, stirring until a dough forms.

5. Shape the dough into small donut rounds or use a silicone donut mold.

6. Lightly spray the air fryer basket with olive oil and place the donuts inside, ensuring they are not touching.

7. Air fry for 8-10 minutes or until golden brown.

8. Allow the donuts to cool slightly before removing them from the air fryer.

9. Optional: Dust with extra erythritol or drizzle with a keto-friendly glaze for added sweetness.

Cinnamon Churro Bites

Time: 20 minutes	Serving Size: 4 servings
Prep Time: 10 minutes	Cook Time: 10 minutes

Nutrition Information Per Serving (1 serving unit):
Calories: 160, Carbohydrates: 5g, Saturated Fat: 6g, Protein: 6g, Fat: 13g, Sodium: 90mg, Potassium: 80mg, Fiber: 3g, Sugar: 1g, Vitamin C: 0mg, Calcium: 35mg, Iron: 1mg.

Ingredients:

- 1 cup almond flour
- 2 tbsps coconut flour
- 1 tbsp powdered erythritol (or preferred keto sweetener)
- 1/2 tsp ground cinnamon
- 1/2 tsp baking powder
- 1/4 cup unsweetened
- almond milk
- 2 large eggs
- 2 tbsps melted butter
- 1 tsp vanilla extract
- 1/4 cup erythritol and 1/2 tsp cinnamon for coating
- Olive oil spray (for greasing the air fryer)

Directions:

1. Preheat the air fryer to 350°F.
2. In a medium bowl, mix the almond flour, coconut flour, powdered erythritol, cinnamon, and baking powder.
3. In another bowl, whisk together eggs, melted butter, almond milk, and vanilla extract.
4. Slowly incorporate the wet ingredients into the dry ingredients, mixing until a dough forms.
5. Roll the dough into small bite-sized balls or logs.
6. Lightly spray the air fryer basket with olive oil and place the churro bites inside, ensuring they are spaced apart. Air fry for 8-10 minutes or until golden brown.
7. While the churro bites are cooking, mix the erythritol and cinnamon for the coating.
8. Once done, remove the churro bites and immediately toss them in the cinnamon-erythritol mixture for a sweet and spicy coating.

Air-Fried Cheesecake Bites

Time: 35 minutes	Serving Size: 4 cheesecake bites
Prep Time: 15 minutes	Cook Time: 20 minutes

Nutrition Information Per Serving (1 cheesecake bite):
Calories: 220, Carbohydrates: 4g, Saturated Fat: 10g, Protein: 6g, Fat: 19g, Sodium: 130mg, Potassium: 70mg, Fiber: 1g, Sugar: 1g, Vitamin C: 0mg, Calcium: 35mg, Iron: 0.5mg.

Ingredients:

- 8 oz cream cheese, softened
- 1/4 cup powdered erythritol (or preferred keto sweetener)
- 1 large egg
- 1 tsp vanilla extract
- 1 tbsp coconut flour
- 1/2 tsp lemon zest
- 1/4 cup almond flour
- 2 tbsps melted butter
- 1/4 tsp ground cinnamon
- Olive oil spray (for greasing the air fryer)

Directions:

1. Preheat the air fryer to 320°F.
2. In a medium bowl, beat the cream cheese, erythritol, egg, vanilla extract, and lemon zest until smooth and creamy.
3. Add the coconut flour to the mixture and blend until fully incorporated.
4. In a separate small bowl, mix the almond flour, melted butter, and ground cinnamon to form a crumbly texture. This will be your crust.
5. Grease a silicone muffin mold or individual small ramekins with olive oil spray.
6. Press a small amount of the almond flour crust into the bottom of each mold or ramekin.
7. Pour the cheesecake batter evenly over the crusts.
8. Place the molds or ramekins in the air fryer and cook for 18-20 minutes until the cheesecake is set and slightly golden on top.
9. Remove and let the cheesecake bites cool to room temperature, then refrigerate for at least 1 hour before serving.

Keto Chocolate Lava Cakes

 Time:
25 minutes

 Serving Size:
4 cakes

 Prep Time:
10 minutes

 Cook Time:
15 minutes

Nutrition Information Per Serving (1 cake):
Calories: 240, Carbohydrates: 6g, Saturated Fat: 12g, Protein: 7g, Fat: 21g, Sodium: 150mg, Potassium: 180mg, Fiber: 4g, Sugar: 1g, Vitamin C: 0mg, Calcium: 30mg, Iron: 2mg.

Ingredients:
- 1/2 cup unsweetened dark chocolate (70% cocoa or higher), chopped
- 1/4 cup unsalted butter
- 2 large eggs
- 1/4 cup powdered erythritol (or preferred keto sweetener)
- 1 tsp vanilla extract
- 2 tbsps almond flour
- 1 tbsp cocoa powder
- Pinch of sea salt
- Olive oil spray (for greasing the ramekins)

Directions:
1. Preheat the air fryer to 350°F.
2. In a microwave-safe bowl, melt the chopped dark chocolate and butter together in 30-second intervals, stirring in between, until smooth. Set aside to cool slightly.
3. In a separate bowl, whisk the eggs, powdered erythritol, and vanilla extract until light and frothy.
4. Gradually fold the melted chocolate mixture into the egg mixture, stirring until combined.
5. Add the almond flour, cocoa powder, and a pinch of sea salt, stirring gently until a smooth batter forms.
6. Grease four small ramekins with olive oil spray and divide the batter evenly among them.
7. Place the ramekins in the air fryer basket and cook for 12-15 minutes until the edges are set but the center remains slightly soft.
8. Carefully remove the ramekins from the air fryer and let them cool for a few minutes before serving.
9. Serve warm for that classic molten lava texture, optionally dusted with additional erythritol or a dollop of whipped cream.

Lemon Ricotta Air-Fried Pancakes

 Time:
20 minutes

 Serving Size:
6 pancakes

 Prep Time:
10 minutes

 Cook Time:
10 minutes

Nutrition Information Per Serving (1 pancake):
Calories: 150, Carbohydrates: 5g, Saturated Fat: 6g, Protein: 9g, Fat: 12g, Sodium: 220mg, Potassium: 90mg, Fiber: 2g, Sugar: 1g, Vitamin C: 4mg, Calcium: 120mg, Iron: 1mg.

Ingredients:
- 1/2 cup ricotta cheese
- 2 large eggs
- 1 tbsp lemon zest
- 1 tbsp lemon juice
- 1/4 cup almond flour
- 1 tbsp coconut flour
- 1 tsp baking powder
- 1 tbsp powdered erythritol (or preferred keto sweetener)
- 1/4 tsp vanilla extract
- Olive oil spray (for greasing the air fryer basket)

Directions:
1. Preheat the air fryer to 340°F.
2. In a medium bowl, whisk together ricotta cheese, eggs, lemon zest, and lemon juice until smooth and creamy.
3. In a separate bowl, combine almond flour, coconut flour, baking powder, and powdered erythritol.
4. Gradually add the dry ingredients to the ricotta mixture, stirring until fully combined. Add vanilla extract and mix well.
5. Lightly grease the air fryer basket with olive oil spray.
6. Scoop 2-3 tbsp-sized portions of the batter into the air fryer basket, flattening them gently with the back of a spoon to form pancake shapes.
7. Cook for 8-10 minutes, flipping halfway through, until the pancakes are golden brown and cooked through.
8. Remove the pancakes from the air fryer and let cool for a few minutes before serving.
9. Serve warm, optionally with whipped cream or a sprinkle of lemon zest for extra flavor.

Keto Brownie Bites

Time: 25 minutes	Serving Size: 6 brownie bites
Prep Time: 10 minutes	Cook Time: 15 minutes

Nutrition Information Per Serving (1 brownie bite):

Calories: 160, Carbohydrates: 5g, Saturated Fat: 4g, Protein: 4g, Fat: 14g, Sodium: 50mg, Potassium: 80mg, Fiber: 3g, Sugar: 1g, Vitamin C: 0%, Calcium: 2%, Iron: 6%.

Ingredients:

- 1/2 cup almond flour
- 1/4 cup unsweetened cocoa powder
- 1/4 cup keto-friendly sweetener (e.g., erythritol)
- 1/4 cup butter, melted
- 2 large eggs
- 1 tsp vanilla extract
- 1/2 tsp baking powder
- Pinch of salt
- Optional: 2 tbsp sugar-free chocolate chips

Directions:

1. Preheat the air fryer to 350°F.
2. In a medium bowl, combine almond flour, cocoa powder, keto-friendly sweetener, baking powder, and salt.
3. In another bowl, whisk together the eggs, melted butter, and vanilla extract.
4. Gradually fold the dry ingredients into the wet ingredients until well combined. Stir in optional sugar-free chocolate chips if desired.
5. Using a spoon, divide the batter into small silicone muffin molds or a greased air fryer-safe tray, filling each about halfway.
6. Air-fry for 10-15 minutes or until a toothpick inserted into the center comes out clean.
7. Let cool for a few minutes before removing from molds and serving.

Cinnamon Sugar Almond Flour Pastry Twists

Time: 30 minutes	Serving Size: 8 pastry twists
Prep Time: 10 minutes	Cook Time: 20 minutes

Nutrition Information Per Serving (1 pastry twist):

Calories: 120, Carbohydrates: 4g, Saturated Fat: 2g, Protein: 4g, Fat: 10g, Sodium: 60mg, Potassium: 70mg, Fiber: 2g, Sugar: 1g, Vitamin C: 0%, Calcium: 4%, Iron: 6%.

Ingredients:

- 1 1/4 cups almond flour
- 1/4 cup keto-friendly sweetener (such as erythritol)
- 2 tbsp melted butter
- 1 large egg
- 1 tsp vanilla extract
- 1/2 tsp baking powder
- 1/2 tsp cinnamon
- Pinch of salt
- 1 tsp cinnamon mixed with 1 tbsp keto-friendly sweetener for topping

Directions:

1. Preheat your air fryer to 350°F.
2. In a medium bowl, combine almond flour, keto-friendly sweetener, baking powder, cinnamon, and salt.
3. In a separate bowl, whisk together the melted butter, egg, and vanilla extract until smooth.
4. Gradually add the dry ingredients to the wet mixture and stir until a dough forms.
5. Roll the dough into small logs (about 4 inches long) and gently twist each log to form the pastry twists.
6. Place the twists into the air fryer basket lined with parchment paper, ensuring they do not touch.
7. Air fry for 12-15 minutes or until golden brown and crisp on the edges.
8. Remove from the air fryer, brush with a bit of melted butter, and sprinkle with the cinnamon-sweetener topping mixture.
9. Allow to cool slightly before serving.

Air-Fried Berry Crumble

 Time:
25 minutes

 Serving Size:
4 bowls

 Prep Time:
10 minutes

 Cook Time:
15 minutes

Nutrition Information Per Serving (1 bowl):
Calories: 180, Carbohydrates: 8g, Saturated Fat: 4g, Protein: 5g, Fat: 14g, Sodium: 50mg, Potassium: 130mg, Fiber: 4g, Sugar: 3g, Vitamin C: 15%, Calcium: 6%, Iron: 8%.

Ingredients:

- 1 cup mixed berries (blueberries, raspberries, and strawberries)
- 1/2 cup almond flour
- 1/4 cup chopped pecans
- 2 tbsp coconut flour
- 3 tbsp melted butter
- 2 tbsp keto-friendly sweetener (such as erythritol)
- 1 tsp vanilla extract
- 1/2 tsp cinnamon
- Pinch of salt

Directions:

1. Preheat your air fryer to 350°F.
2. In a small bowl, toss the mixed berries with 1 tbsp of the keto-friendly sweetener and set aside.
3. In another bowl, mix the almond flour, coconut flour, chopped pecans, the remaining sweetener, cinnamon, and a pinch of salt.
4. Add the melted butter and vanilla extract to the dry mixture, stirring until crumbly.
5. Divide the berries evenly into four small ramekins, then top each with the crumble mixture.
6. Place the ramekins into the air fryer and cook for 12-15 minutes, or until the crumble is golden brown and the berries are bubbling.
7. Remove from the air fryer and allow to cool slightly before serving.

Keto Apple Cinnamon «Faux» Rings

 Time:
20 minutes

 Serving Size:
4 rings

Prep Time:
10 minutes

Cook Time:
10 minutes

Nutrition Information Per Serving (1 ring):
Calories: 120, Carbohydrates: 6g, Saturated Fat: 2g, Protein: 3g, Fat: 9g, Sodium: 50mg, Potassium: 95mg, Fiber: 4g, Sugar: 1g, Vitamin C: 8%, Calcium: 4%, Iron: 5%.

Ingredients:

- 2 medium zucchini, peeled and sliced into 1/4-inch thick rings
- 2 tbsp almond flour
- 1 tbsp coconut flour
- 2 tbsp unsweetened almond milk
- 1 large egg
- 1 tbsp keto-friendly
- sweetener (erythritol or monk fruit)
- 1 tsp ground cinnamon
- 1/4 tsp ground nutmeg
- 1/2 tsp vanilla extract
- Coconut oil spray

Directions:

1. Preheat your air fryer to 350°F.
2. In a small bowl, whisk the egg, almond milk, vanilla extract, sweetener, cinnamon, and nutmeg together until well combined.
3. In a separate shallow dish, combine the almond flour and coconut flour.
4. Dip each zucchini ring into the egg mixture, then coat it with the flour mixture, shaking off any excess.
5. Lightly spray the air fryer basket with coconut oil spray, then place the coated zucchini rings in a single layer, making sure they don't overlap.
6. Air fry for 8-10 minutes, flipping halfway through, until golden brown and crispy.
7. Once cooked, remove the rings from the air fryer and sprinkle with an additional dusting of cinnamon, if desired.

Keto Chocolate Chip Cookies

 Time:
25 minutes

 Serving Size:
12 cookies

 Prep Time:
10 minutes

 Cook Time:
15 minutes

Nutrition Information Per Serving (1 cookie):
Calories: 120, Carbohydrates: 4g, Saturated Fat: 3g, Protein: 2g, Fat: 10g, Sodium: 90mg, Potassium: 50mg, Fiber: 2g, Sugar: 1g, Vitamin C: 0%, Calcium: 2%, Iron: 4%.

Ingredients:
- 1 cup almond flour
- 1/4 cup coconut flour
- 1/2 cup unsalted butter, softened
- 1/4 cup keto-friendly sweetener (erythritol or monk fruit)
- 1 large egg
- 1 tsp vanilla extract
- 1/2 tsp baking powder
- 1/4 tsp salt
- 1/3 cup sugar-free chocolate chips

Directions:
1. Preheat your air fryer to 320°F.
2. In a medium bowl, cream together the softened butter and keto-friendly sweetener until smooth and fluffy.
3. Add the egg and vanilla extract, mixing until well combined.
4. In another bowl, whisk together the almond flour, coconut flour, baking powder, and salt. Gradually add the dry ingredients to the wet mixture, stirring until a dough forms.
5. Fold in the sugar-free chocolate chips.
6. Roll the dough into small balls and slightly flatten them. Place the dough balls in the air fryer basket, leaving space between each cookie.
7. Air fry for 10-12 minutes, or until the edges are golden and the cookies are set.
8. Let the cookies cool for 5 minutes before serving.

Air-Fried Coconut Macaroons

 Time:
20 minutes

 Serving Size:
10 macaroons

 Prep Time:
10 minutes

 Cook Time:
10 minutes

Nutrition Information Per Serving (1 macaroon):
Calories: 90, Carbohydrates: 3g, Saturated Fat: 6g, Protein: 1g, Fat: 8g, Sodium: 30mg, Potassium: 40mg, Fiber: 2g, Sugar: 1g, Vitamin C: 0%, Calcium: 1%, Iron: 2%.

Ingredients:
- 2 cups unsweetened shredded coconut
- 1/4 cup keto-friendly sweetener (erythritol or monk fruit)
- 2 large egg whites
- 1 tsp vanilla extract
- 1/4 tsp almond extract
- 1/8 tsp salt

Directions:
1. Preheat the air fryer to 320°F.
2. In a mixing bowl, whisk the egg whites until they become frothy.
3. Add the keto-friendly sweetener, vanilla extract, almond extract, and salt to the egg whites, and whisk until combined.
4. Gently fold in the shredded coconut until the mixture is fully incorporated and sticky.
5. Using a small cookie scoop or spoon, form the mixture into small mounds and place them in the air fryer basket lined with parchment paper.
6. Air fry for 8-10 minutes, or until the macaroons are golden brown on the edges.
7. Allow the macaroons to cool for 5 minutes before serving.

Keto Peanut Butter Air-Fried Bars

Time: 30 minutes	Serving Size: 8 bars
Prep Time: 10 minutes	Cook Time: 20 minutes

Nutrition Information Per Serving (1 bar):

Calories: 160, Carbohydrates: 4g, Saturated Fat: 3g, Protein: 7g, Fat: 14g, Sodium: 120mg, Potassium: 90mg, Fiber: 2g, Sugar: 1g, Vitamin C: 0%, Calcium: 2%, Iron: 4%.

Ingredients:

- 1 cup creamy unsweetened peanut butter
- 1/4 cup keto-friendly sweetener (such as erythritol)
- 2 large eggs
- 1/4 cup almond flour
- 1/2 tsp vanilla extract
- 1/2 tsp baking powder
- 1/8 tsp salt

Directions:

1. Preheat your air fryer to 320°F.
2. In a large bowl, mix the peanut butter, eggs, keto sweetener, and vanilla extract until smooth and creamy.
3. Add in the almond flour, baking powder, and salt, stirring until the ingredients are fully incorporated and form a thick batter.
4. Lightly grease an air fryer-safe baking dish or line it with parchment paper. Spread the peanut butter batter evenly into the dish.
5. Place the dish in the air fryer and cook for 15-20 minutes or until the top is golden and a toothpick inserted comes out clean.
6. Allow the bars to cool in the dish for 5 minutes before cutting them into squares.

Keto Pecan Pie Bites

Time: 30 minutes	Serving Size: 8 pie bites
Prep Time: 10 minutes	Cook Time: 20 minutes

Nutrition Information Per Serving (1 pie bite):

Calories: 190, Carbohydrates: 4g, Saturated Fat: 3g, Protein: 5g, Fat: 18g, Sodium: 60mg, Potassium: 70mg, Fiber: 2g, Sugar: 1g, Vitamin C: 0%, Calcium: 4%, Iron: 3%.

Ingredients:

- 1 cup pecan halves
- 1/4 cup almond flour
- 2 tbsp coconut flour
- 1/4 cup unsalted butter, melted
- 2 tbsp keto-friendly maple syrup
- 1/2 tsp vanilla extract
- 1/4 tsp ground cinnamon
- Pinch of salt

Directions:

1. Preheat your air fryer to 350°F.
2. In a mixing bowl, combine the almond flour, coconut flour, melted butter, keto maple syrup, vanilla extract, cinnamon, and a pinch of salt. Stir until a dough forms.
3. Press a small amount of dough into mini silicone molds or shape them into bite-sized rounds by hand.
4. Gently press a pecan half into the top of each dough bite.
5. Place the bites in the air fryer and cook for 10-12 minutes, or until golden brown.
6. Allow to cool before removing from the molds or handling. Serve and enjoy!

Air-Fried Lemon Poppy Seed Muffins

⏰ Time: 30 minutes	🍽 Serving Size: 6 muffins
🥗 Prep Time: 10 minutes	👨‍🍳 Cook Time: 20 minutes

Nutrition Information Per Serving (1 muffin):

Calories: 180, Carbohydrates: 5g, Saturated Fat: 3g, Protein: 6g, Fat: 15g, Sodium: 90mg, Potassium: 80mg, Fiber: 3g, Sugar: 1g, Vitamin C: 2%, Calcium: 4%, Iron: 3%.

Ingredients:

- 1 cup almond flour
- 2 tbsp coconut flour
- 2 tbsp poppy seeds
- 1/4 cup unsweetened almond milk
- 1/4 cup melted coconut oil
- 2 large eggs
- Zest and juice of 1 lemon
- 2 tbsp keto-friendly sweetener
- 1 tsp baking powder
- 1/2 tsp vanilla extract
- Pinch of salt

Directions:

1. Preheat your air fryer to 330°F.
2. In a mixing bowl, whisk together the almond flour, coconut flour, poppy seeds, baking powder, and salt.
3. In a separate bowl, beat the eggs, then add the almond milk, coconut oil, lemon zest, lemon juice, sweetener, and vanilla extract. Mix until smooth.
4. Combine the wet ingredients with the dry ingredients, stirring until a batter forms.
5. Pour the batter into silicone muffin molds, filling each about 2/3 full.
6. Place the molds in the air fryer and cook for 15-20 minutes or until golden and a toothpick comes out clean.
7. Let the muffins cool before serving. Enjoy!

Low-Carb Air-Fried Blueberry Turnovers

⏰ Time: 25 minutes	🍽 Serving Size: 4 turnovers
🥗 Prep Time: 10 minutes	👨‍🍳 Cook Time: 15 minutes

Nutrition Information Per Serving (1 turnover):

Calories: 160, Carbohydrates: 7g, Saturated Fat: 4g, Protein: 6g, Fat: 12g, Sodium: 85mg, Potassium: 70mg, Fiber: 3g, Sugar: 2g, Vitamin C: 4%, Calcium: 5%, Iron: 2%.

Ingredients:

- 1/2 cup almond flour
- 1/4 cup coconut flour
- 2 tbsp keto-friendly sweetener
- 1/4 cup cold unsalted butter, cubed
- 1 large egg
- 2 tbsp cream cheese, softened
- 1/2 cup fresh blueberries
- 1 tsp lemon zest
- 1/4 tsp vanilla extract
- Pinch of salt

Directions:

1. Preheat your air fryer to 350°F.
2. In a bowl, mix the almond flour, coconut flour, sweetener, and salt. Add the cold butter cubes and work them into the flour mixture using your fingers until it resembles coarse crumbs.
3. In a separate bowl, whisk the egg and vanilla extract, then add to the flour mixture. Stir until a dough forms.
4. Divide the dough into 4 portions and flatten each into a small disk.
5. In another bowl, combine the cream cheese, blueberries, and lemon zest.
6. Spoon a small amount of the blueberry mixture into the center of each dough disk. Fold the dough over and press the edges to seal.
7. Place the turnovers in the air fryer and cook for 10-12 minutes or until golden brown.
8. Let cool slightly before serving. Enjoy your low-carb blueberry turnovers!

Chapter 10: 28-Day Meal Prep Plan

Week	Day	Breakfast	Lunch	Snack or appetizer	Dinner
Week 1:	1	Cheesy Bacon Egg Cups	Herb-Crusted Chicken Thighs with Spicy Jalapeño Cauliflower Rice	Parmesan Zucchini Fries	Keto Bacon Cheeseburger Sliders
	2	Air-Fried Avocado Boats with Eggs	Air-Fried Pork Belly Bites with Air-Fried Brussels Sprouts with Bacon	Bacon-Wrapped Jalapeño Poppers	Lemon Dill Salmon Fillets with Roasted Garlic Cauliflower Mash
	3	Keto Sausage Breakfast Balls	Air-Fried Chicken Cordon Bleu with Crispy Air-Fried Radishes	Garlic Butter Shrimp Skewers	Keto Beef Kabobs with Keto «Breaded» Green Beans
	4	Zucchini and Bacon Fritters	Rosemary Lamb Chops with Cheesy Broccoli Bites	Spicy Air-Fried Pickle Chips	Air-Fried Crab Cakes with Avocado Stuffed with Creamy Crab
	5	Almond Flour Pancakes	Keto Chicken Fajita Bowls	Air-Fried Kale Chips	Keto Pork Rind-Crusted Pork Chops with Cabbage and Bacon Crisps
	6	Chorizo and Egg-Stuffed Mushrooms	Spicy Beef Empanadas with Roasted Garlic Cauliflower Bites	Cauliflower and Bacon Mini Tacos	Cajun Shrimp Skewers with Zucchini Lasagna Rolls
	7	Crispy Keto Hash Browns	Mediterranean Stuffed Chicken with Air-Fried Artichoke Hearts	Keto Eggplant Fries	Keto BBQ Pulled Pork with Zucchini Parmesan Crisps
Week 2:	8	Spinach and Cheese Omelette Bites	Air-Fried Bacon-Wrapped Meatloaf with Air-Fried Eggplant Rounds	Spinach and Artichoke Air-Fried Balls	Air-Fried Calamari Rings with Garlic Parmesan Asparagus Spears
	9	Cauliflower Breakfast Skillet	Buffalo Chicken Bites with Keto Cheddar Zucchini Cakes	Crispy Keto Mozzarella Sticks	Air-Fried Garlic Butter Lobster Tails with Spiced Cabbage Steaks
	10	Keto French Toast Sticks	Air-Fried Chicken Meatballs with Keto Avocado Salad Cups	Air-Fried Pork Belly Crisps	Keto Smoked Salmon Avocado Boats with Zucchini Noodles with Pesto
	11	Air-Fried Veggie Frittata	Rosemary and Garlic Chicken Thighs with Air-Fried Brussels Sprout Chips	Avocado Fries with Chipotle Mayo	Spicy Air-Fried Chicken Nuggets with Air-Fried Tofu with Chili Lime
	12	Ham and Cheese Egg Muffins	Keto Chicken Florentine with Air-Fried Mushrooms with Thyme	Cream Cheese Stuffed Mini Bell Peppers	Crispy Pork Schnitzel with Cauliflower Mac and Cheese
	13	Breakfast Sausage Patties	Blackened Shrimp Lettuce Wraps with Grilled Portobello Mushroom Caps	Air-Fried Chicken Tenders	Herb Butter Scallops with Air-Fried Eggplant Parmesan
	14	Keto Breakfast «Burrito» Bowls	Air-Fried Chicken Drumsticks with Air-Fried Spaghetti Squash Boats	Keto Cheddar Biscuits	Air-Fried Beef Ribs with Spicy Jalapeño Cauliflower Rice

Day	Day	Breakfast	Lunch	Snack or appetizer	Dinner
Week 3:	15	Air-Fried Salmon and Spinach Scramble	Keto Beef and Broccoli Skewers with Avocado Stuffed with Creamy Crab	Keto Buffalo Cauliflower Bites	Air-Fried Clams with Garlic Butter with Stuffed Bell Peppers with Cauliflower Rice
	16	Cheesy Bacon Egg Cups	Air-Fried Chicken Fajita Bowls with Crispy Air-Fried Radishes	Spicy Air-Fried Pickle Chips	Keto Coconut Shrimp with Crispy Cauliflower Steaks
	17	Air-Fried Avocado Boats with Eggs	Spicy Tuna Patties with Air-Fried Brussels Sprout Chips	Cauliflower and Bacon Mini Tacos	Italian Sausage-Stuffed Peppers
	18	Keto Sausage Breakfast Balls	Crispy Lemon Garlic Chicken Wings	Air-Fried Kale Chips	Garlic Butter Ribeye Steaks with Air-Fried Stuffed Avocados
	19	Zucchini and Bacon Fritters	Bacon-Wrapped Stuffed Chicken Breastss	Garlic Butter Shrimp Skewers	Parmesan-Crusted Cod with Cabbage and Bacon Crisps
	20	Almond Flour Pancakes	Cajun Chicken Tenders with Air-Fried Artichoke Hearts	Air-Fried Mozzarella Sticks	Mediterranean Stuffed Chicken
	21	Chorizo and Egg-Stuffed Mushrooms	Spicy Beef Empanadas with Air-Fried Brussels Sprouts with Bacon	Cream Cheese Stuffed Mini Bell Peppers	Air-Fried Garlic Butter Lobster Tails with Zucchini Lasagna Rolls
Week 4:	22	Crispy Keto Hash Browns	Rosemary Lamb Chops with Garlic Parmesan Asparagus Spears	Keto Eggplant Fries	Keto Fish Tacos (Cabbage Shells) with Keto Cheddar Zucchini Cakes
	23	Spinach and Cheese Omelette Bites	Air-Fried Bacon-Wrapped Meatloaf with Zucchini Noodles with Pesto	Air-Fried Pork Belly Crisps	Keto Chicken Parmesan with Spiced Cabbage Steaks
	24	Cauliflower Breakfast Skillet	Keto Beef Kabobs with Air-Fried Mushrooms with Thyme	Crispy Keto Mozzarella Sticks	Air-Fried Crab Cakes with Garlic Parmesan Asparagus Spears
	25	Keto French Toast Sticks	Sesame Ginger Chicken Skewers with Keto «Breaded» Green Beans	Bacon-Wrapped Jalapeño Poppers	Keto Coconut Shrimp with Roasted Garlic Cauliflower Bites
	26	Air-Fried Veggie Frittata	Herb-Crusted Rack of Lamb with Crispy Cauliflower Tots	Avocado Fries with Chipotle Mayo	Air-Fried Beef Ribs with Cheesy Broccoli Bites
	27	Ham and Cheese Egg Muffins	Crispy Keto Fish Sticks with Cauliflower Mac and Cheese	Keto Buffalo Cauliflower Bites	Parmesan-Crusted Cod with Roasted Garlic Cauliflower Mash
	28	Breakfast Sausage Patties	Zucchini and Crab-Stuffed Mushrooms	Keto Cheddar Biscuits	Crispy Keto Lamb Meatballs

Free Gift

Thank you! Discover your gift inside! Dive into a rich assortment of DASH Diet for Beginners recipes for added inspiration. Gift it or share the PDF effortlessly with friends and family via a single click on WhatsApp or other social platforms. Bon appétit!

Conclusion outline

Embarking on the Keto Air Fryer Diet may seem challenging at first, but it seamlessly combines the benefits of low-carb, high-fat eating with the convenience of air frying. Through this cookbook, I've explored how to create delicious meals that align with keto principles while using the air fryer to save time and reduce unhealthy fats.

The recipes have been designed to help you stay in ketosis, promoting fat-burning without sacrificing flavor. The air fryer has proven itself as an efficient tool for preparing crispy, satisfying meals with minimal effort and oil.

From breakfasts to dinners, snacks, and even desserts, this cookbook has shown that following a keto diet doesn't mean compromising on taste or spending long hours in the kitchen. Additionally, I've emphasized the importance of understanding your macros, staying hydrated, and choosing high-quality fats and proteins for optimal health.

One key advantage of combining keto with air frying is its flexibility. Whether cooking for yourself or others, you can easily adapt the recipes to suit your preferences while maintaining ketogenic guidelines.

As you continue your keto journey, remember to take things step by step. Start with a few recipes, and soon you'll have a repertoire of go-to meals that make keto living both easy and enjoyable.

If you have specific dietary concerns, don't hesitate to consult a healthcare professional. They can help you tailor the keto diet to your individual health needs.

This cookbook is not just a collection of recipes but a guide to a healthier lifestyle. With the help of your air fryer, you'll find that the keto diet can be both fun and sustainable. So, get cooking—your body and taste buds will thank you!

References

American Dietetic Association. (2023). Ketogenic Diet: A Comprehensive Overview. https://www.eatright.org/food/nutrition/healthy-eating/the-ketogenic-diet

Harvard T.H. Chan School of Public Health. (2023). The Truth Behind the Keto Diet. https://www.hsph.harvard.edu/nutritionsource/healthy-weight/diet-reviews/keto-diet/

Mawer, R. (2023). The Ketogenic Diet 101: A Detailed Beginner's Guide. Healthline. https://www.healthline.com/nutrition/ketogenic-diet-101

Ruled.Me. (2023). Complete Guide to the Ketogenic Diet. https://www.ruled.me/guide-keto-diet/

American Heart Association. (2023). Low-Carb Diets and Heart Health. https://www.heart.org/en/healthy-living/healthy-eating/eat-smart/nutrition-basics/low-carb-diets

Cleveland Clinic. (2023). Keto Diet: What to Expect in the First Month. https://health.clevelandclinic.org/keto-diet-plan

Dr. Axe. (2023). Keto Diet: Your Beginner's Guide. https://draxe.com/nutrition/keto-diet/

Perlmutter, D. (2023). The Keto Diet: How It Can Benefit Your Brain. https://www.drperlmutter.com/keto-diet-and-brain-health/

Ketogenic.com. (2023). Keto Air Fryer Recipes. https://ketogenic.com/recipes/keto-air-fryer-recipes

Academy of Nutrition and Dietetics. (2023). Ketogenic Diet: Understanding the Benefits and Risks. https://www.eatright.org/health/diseases-and-conditions/diabetes/keto-diet-and-diabetes

Johns Hopkins Medicine. (2023). Ketogenic Diet for Epilepsy. https://www.hopkinsmedicine.org/neurology_neurosurgery/centers_clinics/epilepsy/dietary_therapy/ketogenic_diet.html

Virta Health. (2023). The Science Behind the Ketogenic Diet. https://www.virtahealth.com/keto

Mayo Clinic. (2023). Ketogenic Diet: Is the High-Fat, Low-Carb Diet Right for You? https://www.mayoclinic.org/healthy-lifestyle/nutrition-and-healthy-eating/expert-answers/what-is-the-keto-diet

KetoConnect. (2023). Air Fryer Keto Recipes for Fast and Delicious Meals. https://www.ketoconnect.net/keto-air-fryer-recipes

Appendix 1: Measurement Conversion Chart

U.S. System	Metric
1 inch	2.54 centimeters
1 fluid ounce	29.57 milliliters
1 pint (16 ounces)	473.18 milliliters, 2 cups
1 quart (32 ounces)	1 liter, 4 cups
1 gallon (128 ounces)	4 liters, 16 cups
1 pound (16 ounces)	437.5 grams (0.4536 kilogram), 473.18 milliliters
1 ounces	2 tablespoons, 28 grams
1 cup (8 ounces)	237 milliliters
1 teaspoon	5 milliliters
1 tablespoon	15 milliliters (3 teaspoons)
Fahrenheit (subtract 32 and divide by 1.8 to get Celsius)	Centigrade (multiply by 1.8 and add 32 to get Fahrenheit)

Appendix 2: Index Recipes

Notes

Made in United States
North Haven, CT
22 February 2025

66094021R00050

Continue exploring a world of quick and tasty meals with
my other books designed to support your ongoing health goals.

Learn more on the author page:

ISBN 9798344223261

Y0-DYB-858

9 798344 223261